ISBN-978-0-9989026-2-3

First Printing, 2019
Printed in the United States of America

Authors Dylan Jackson, Damare Jackson, Devin Amir
Bauldwin, Terrell Washington

Contact @frxshinc for book covers

So Inspired Publishing Co.

www.soinspiredpublishingco.com

Hi my name is Dylan I'm four years old and I'm quite the charmer and character and I'm a daddy's boy

Hi my name is Damare I'm nine years old and I'm bilingual I speak Chinese and I'm into sports and I'm a daddy's boy

Hi my name is Devin Amir I'm ten years old and I'm a small business owner of a bee hive honey company called The bruthas Bee Farm and I'm a daddy's boy

Hi my name is Terrell and I'm a rapper and straight A student and I'm a daddy's boy

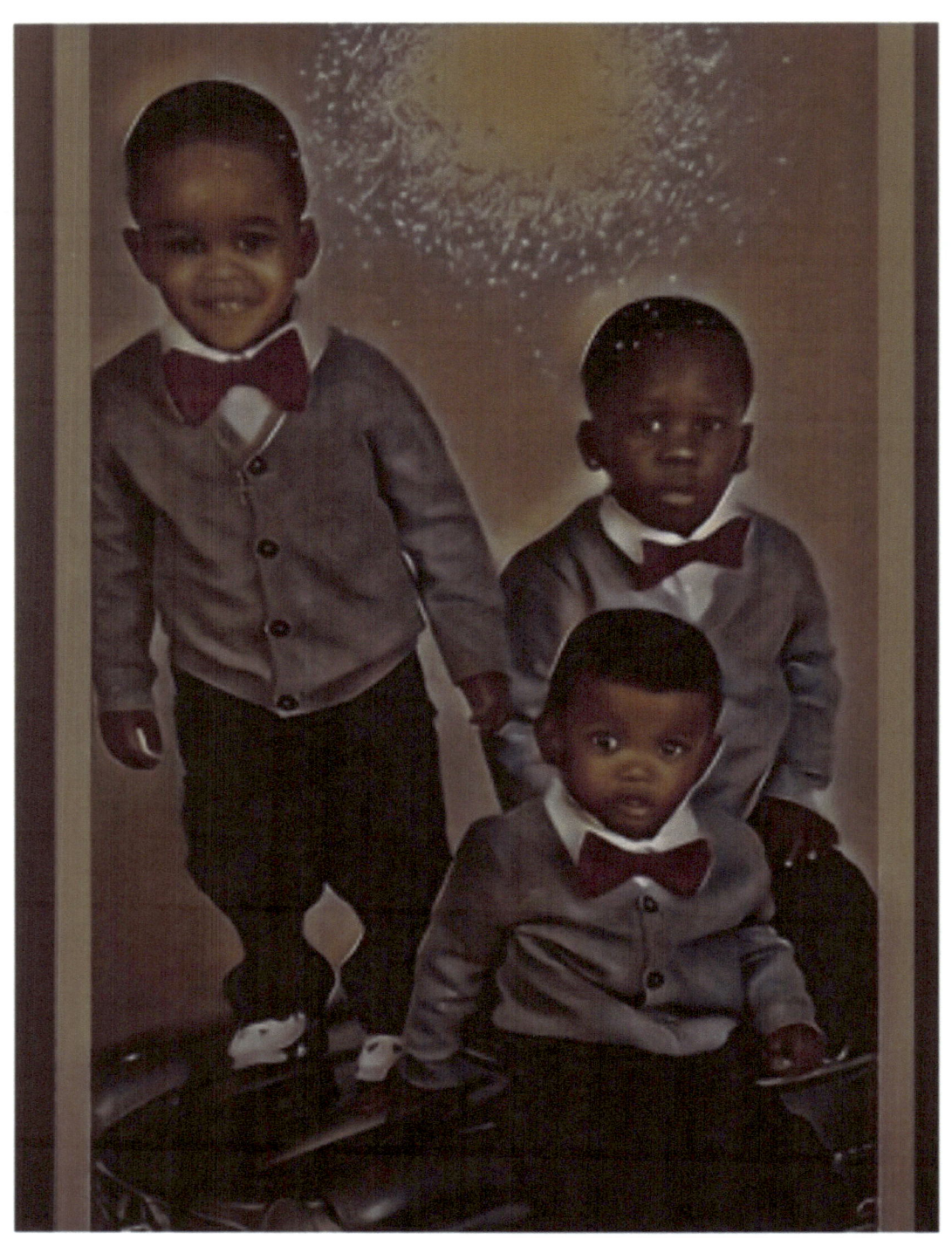

There was just the three of us before there was four (cousins)

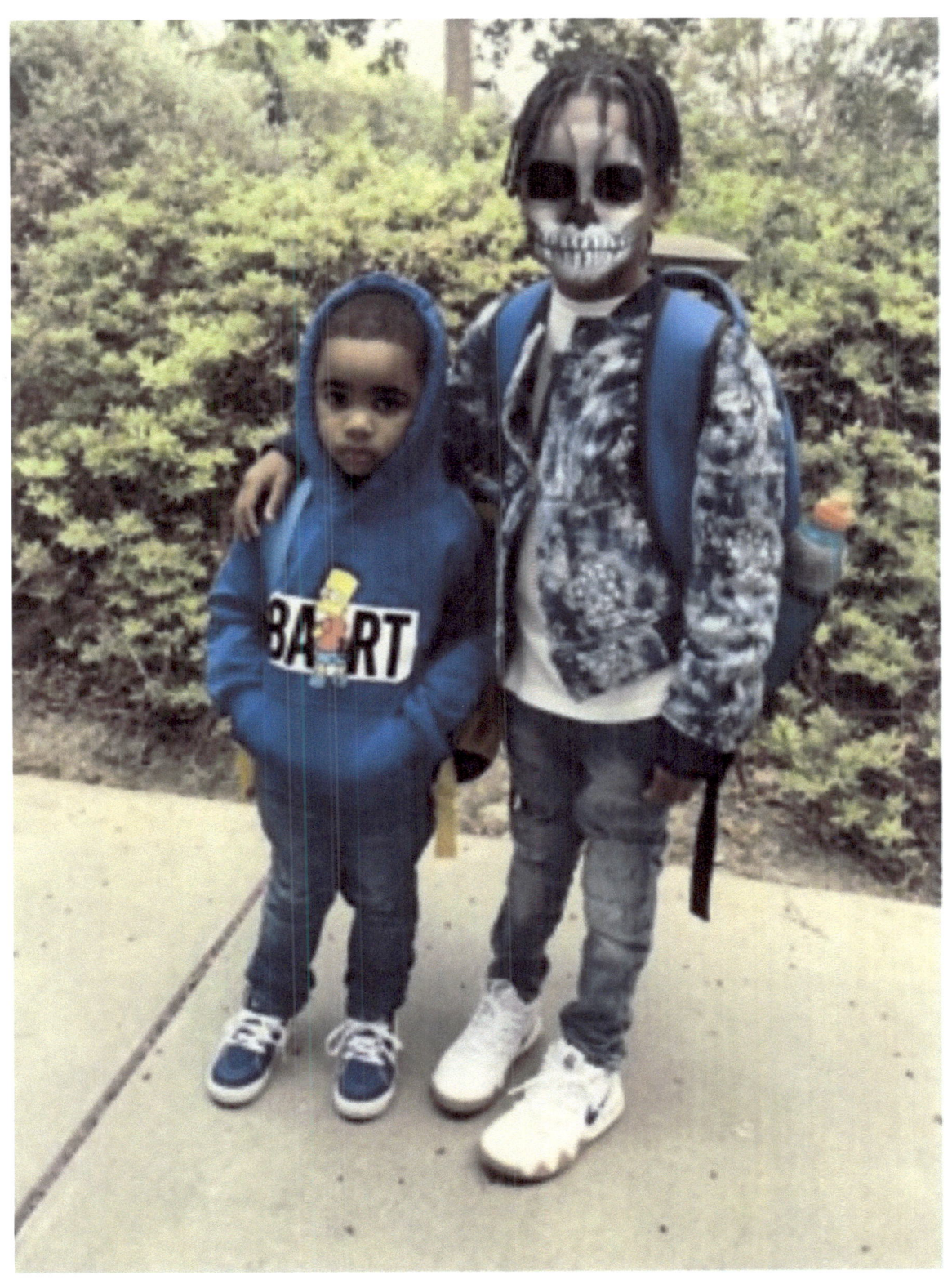

Oh don't mind us we chilling

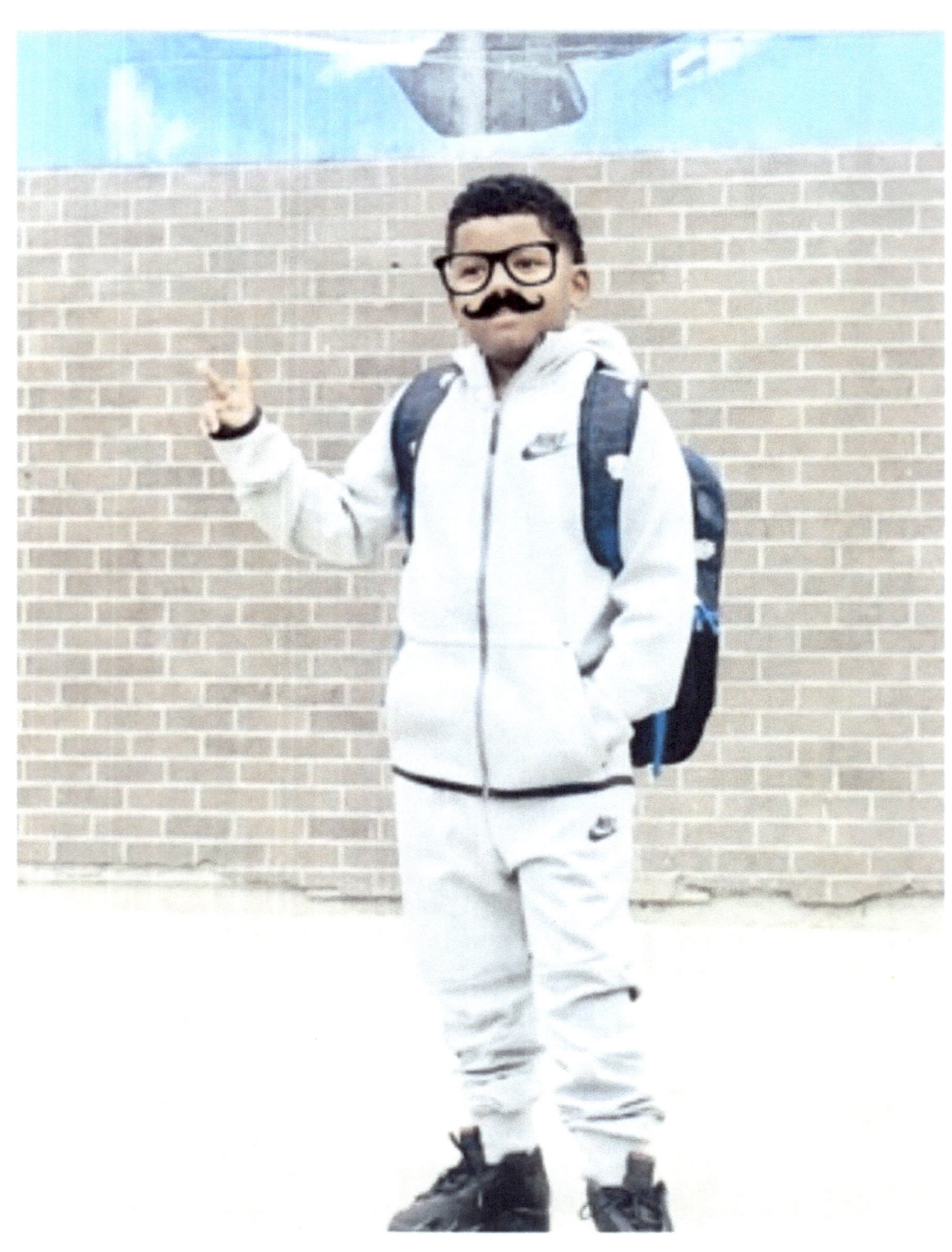

What's up everyone

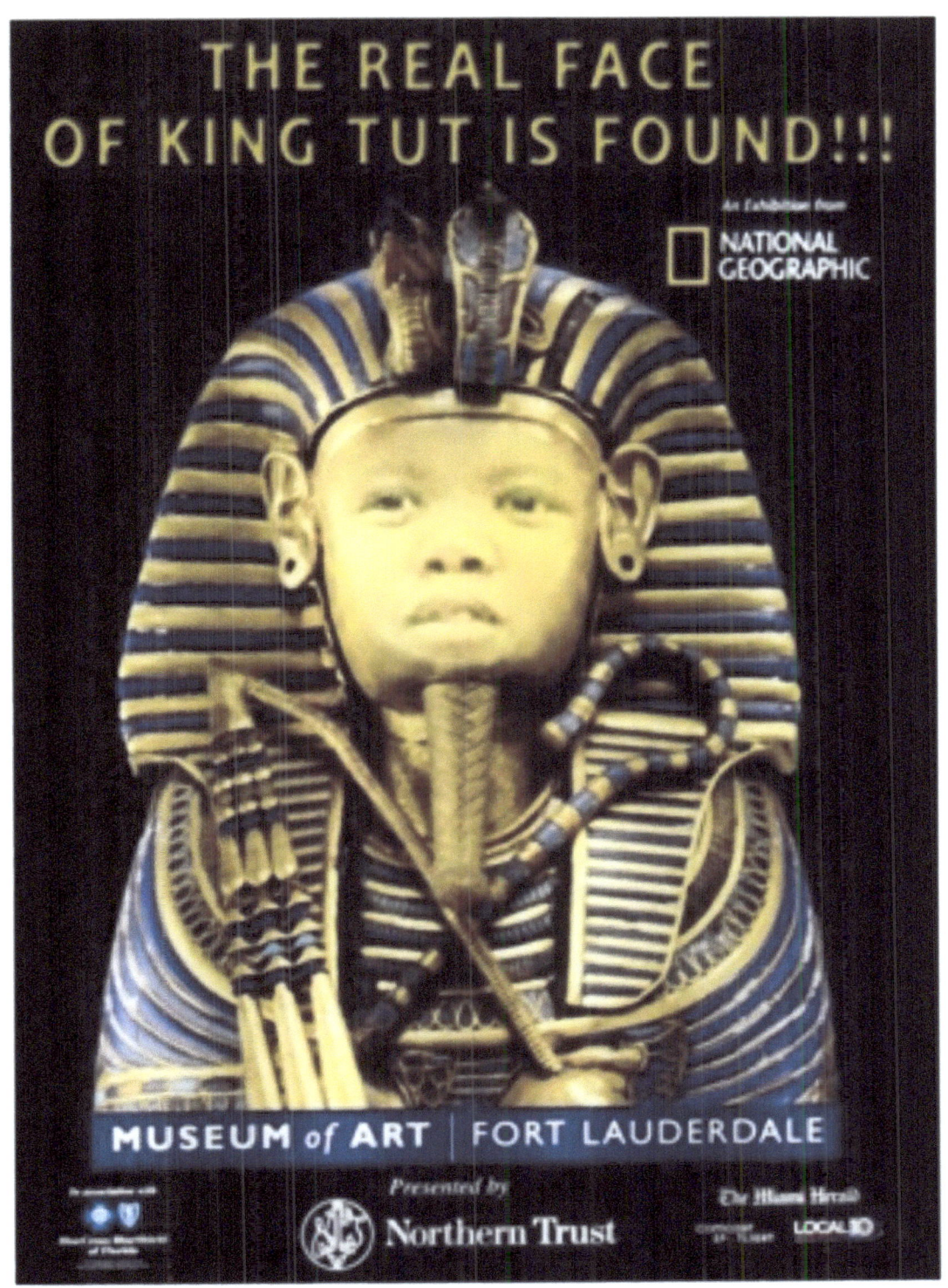

History in the making

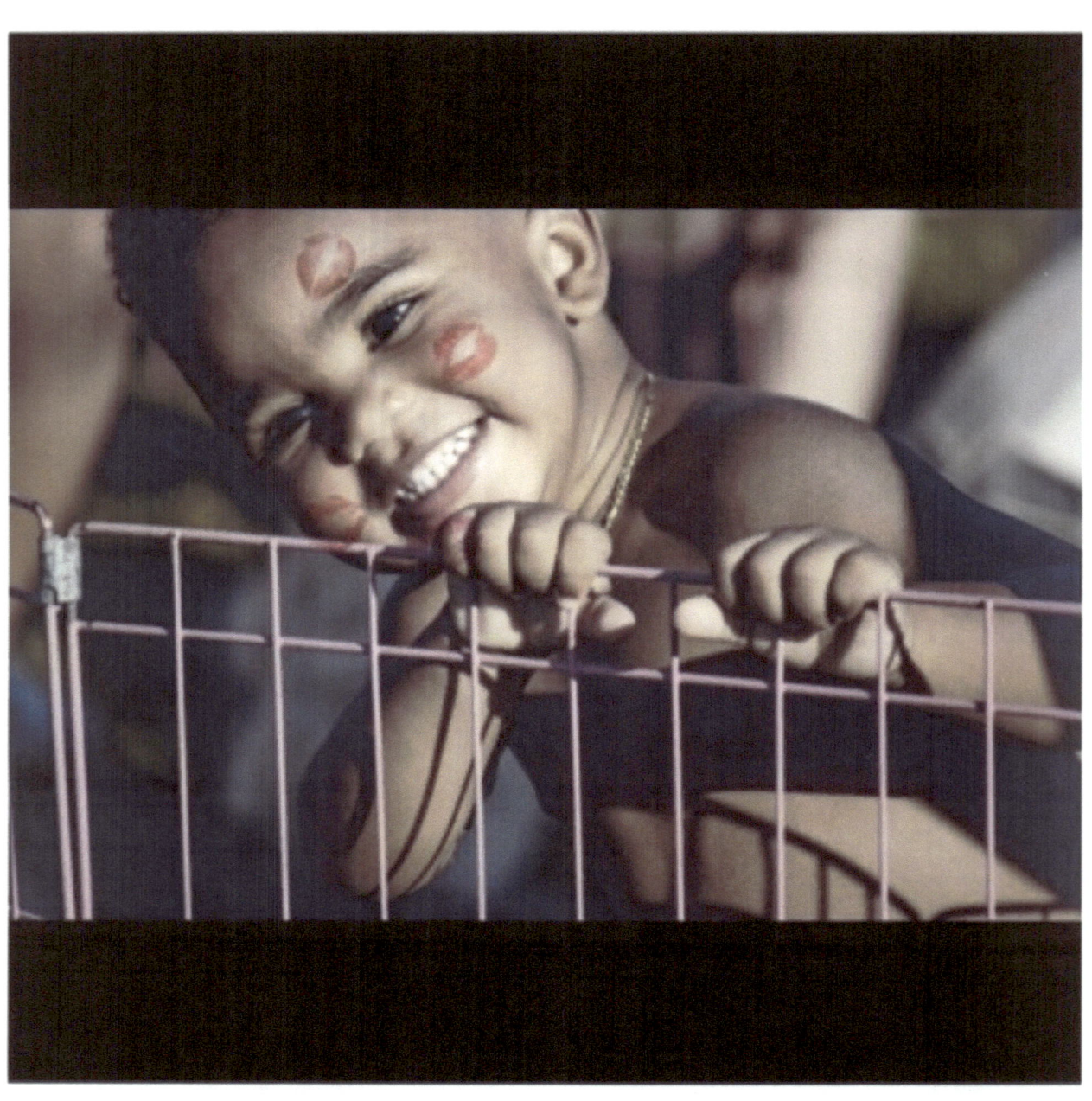

All smiles over here

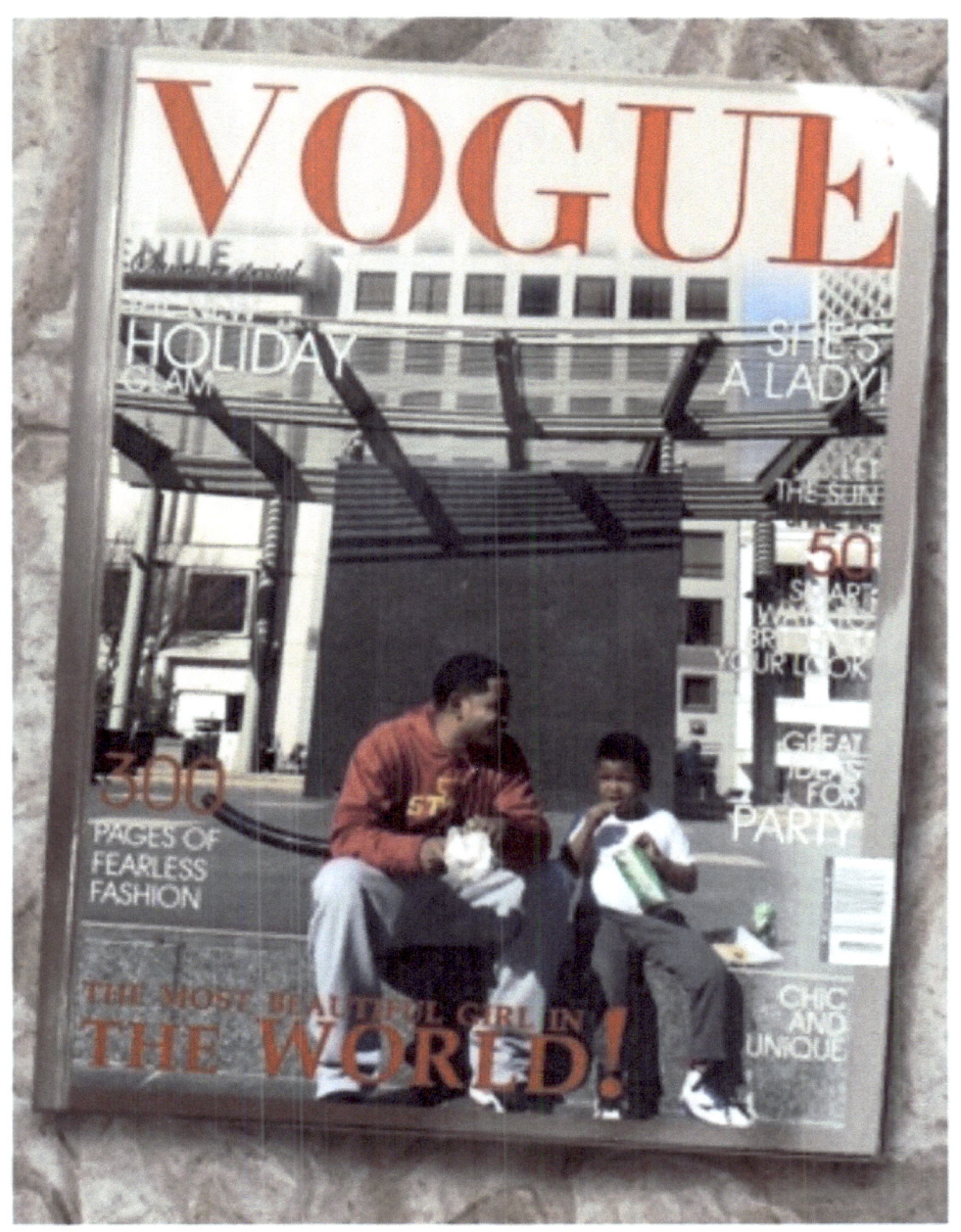

Dad: what you want to be son when you grow up? Son: Like you dad

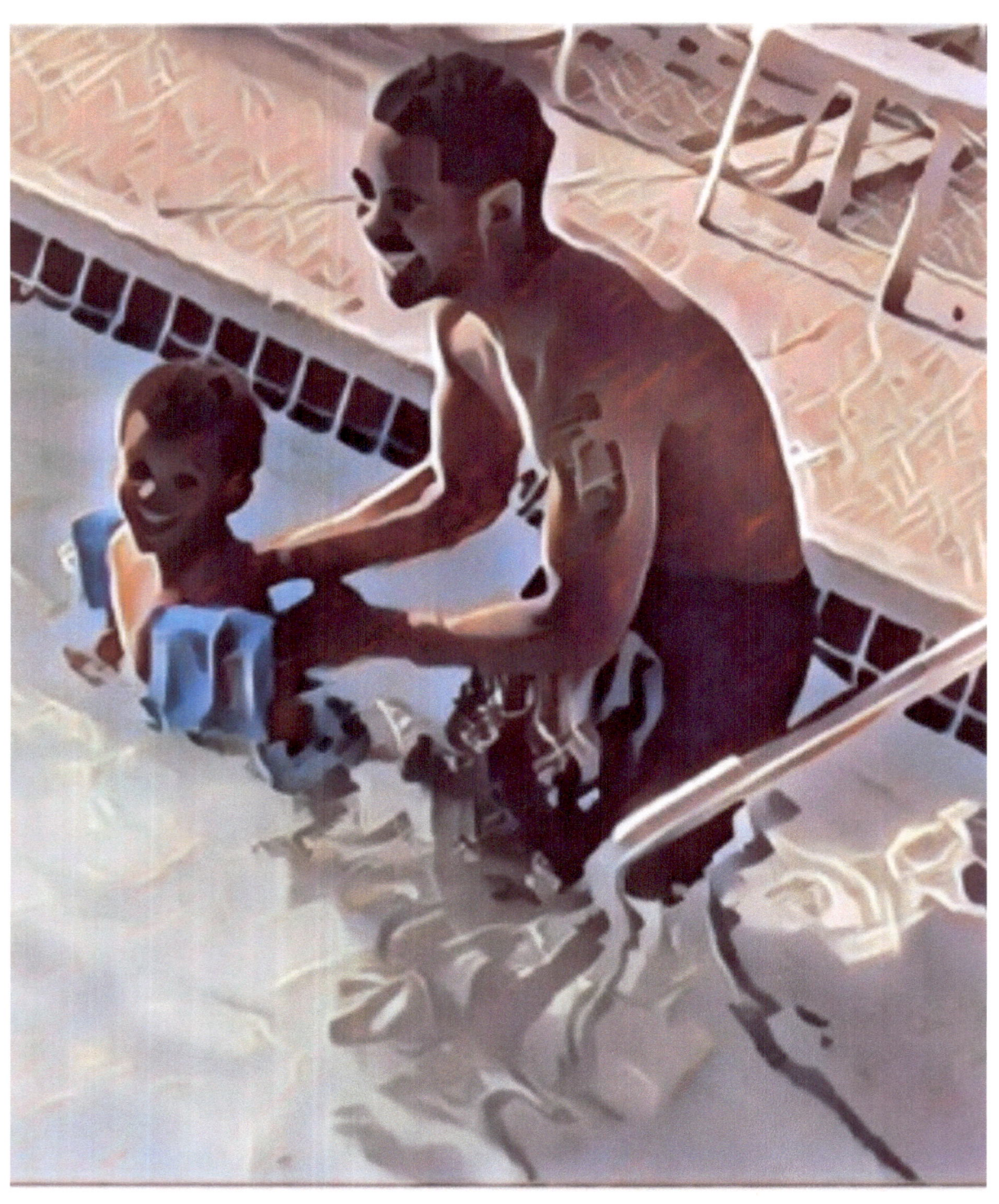

Just chilling

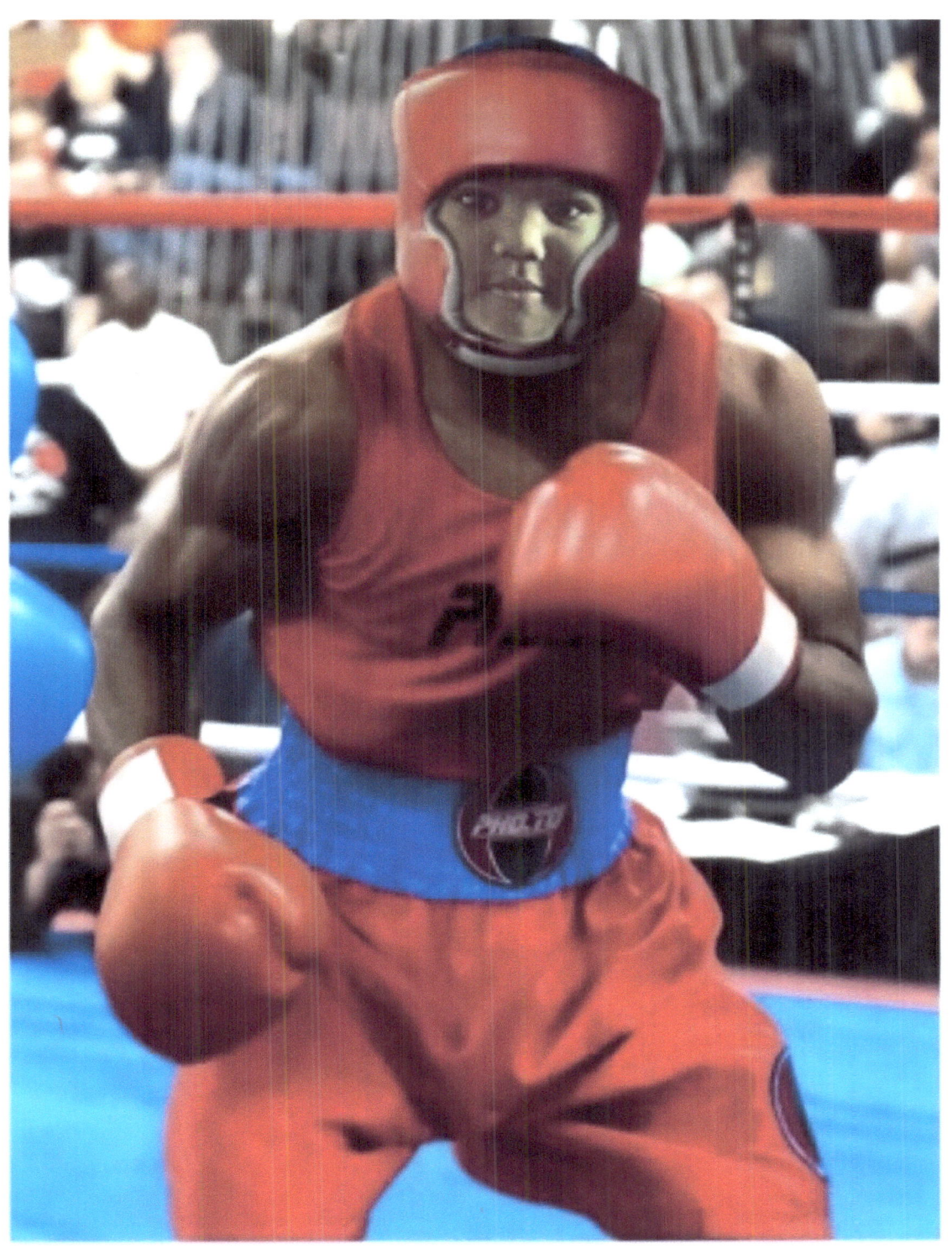

Step into the ring

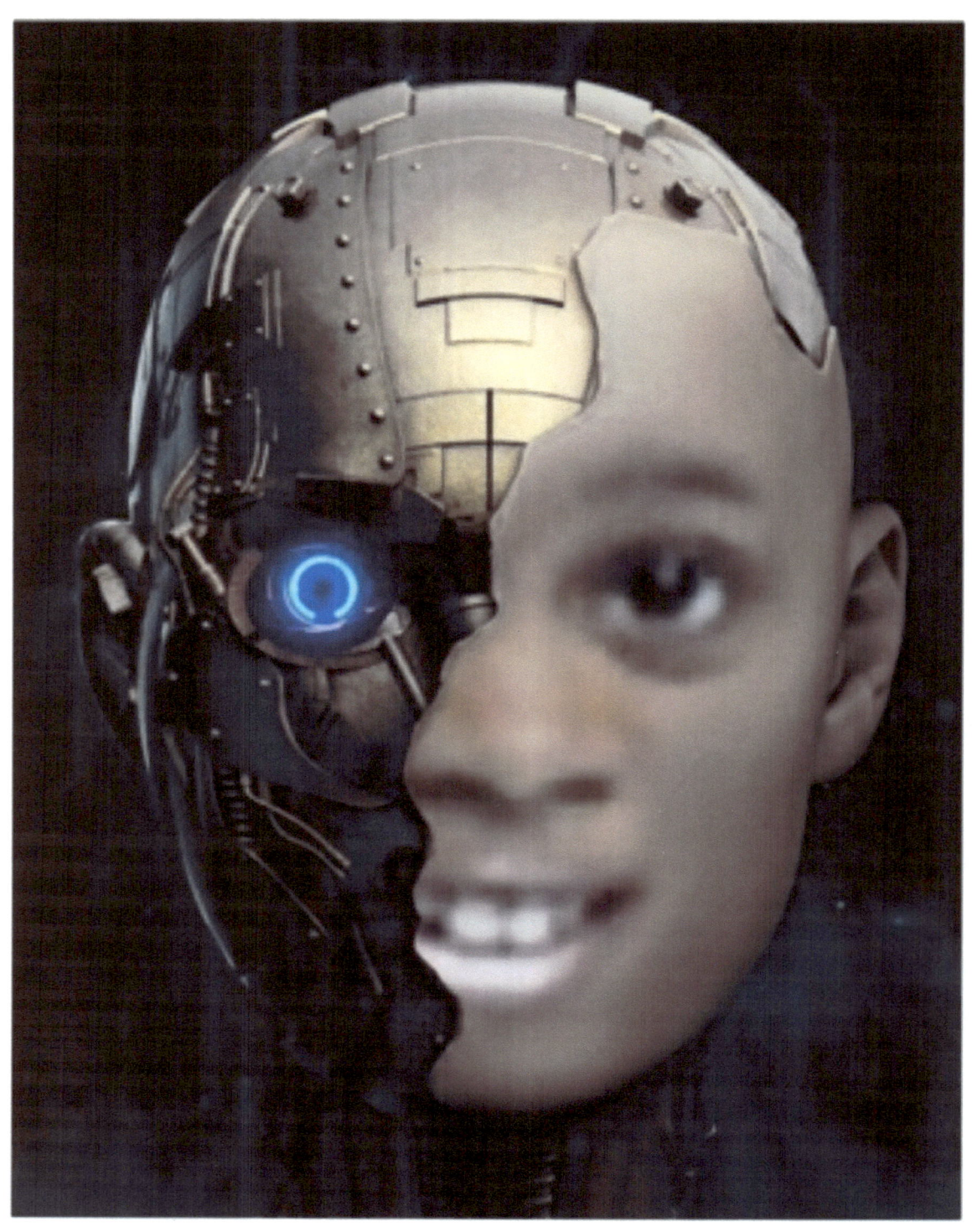

I'm bilingual no really I am

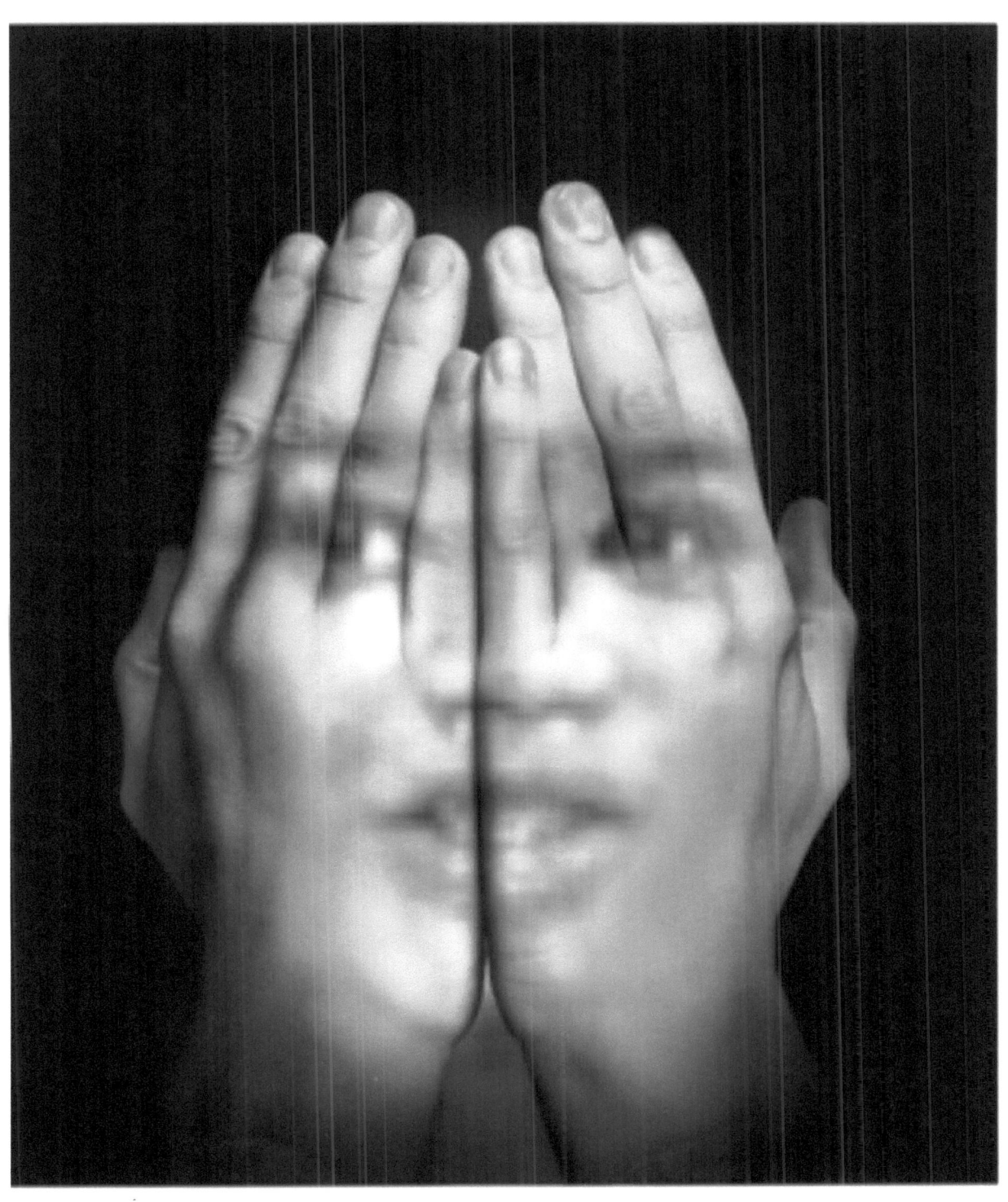

Peek a boo I see you

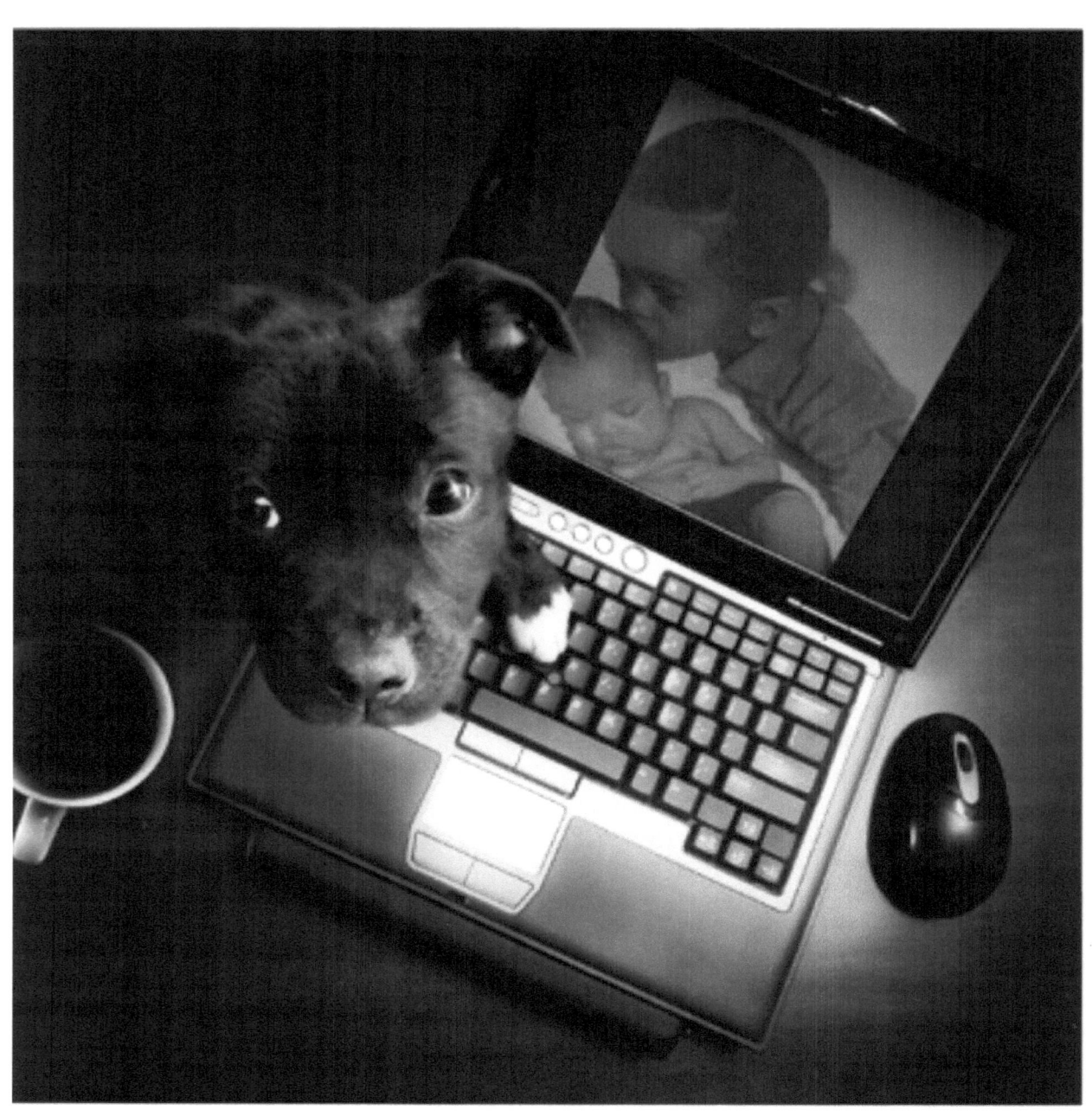

Awe

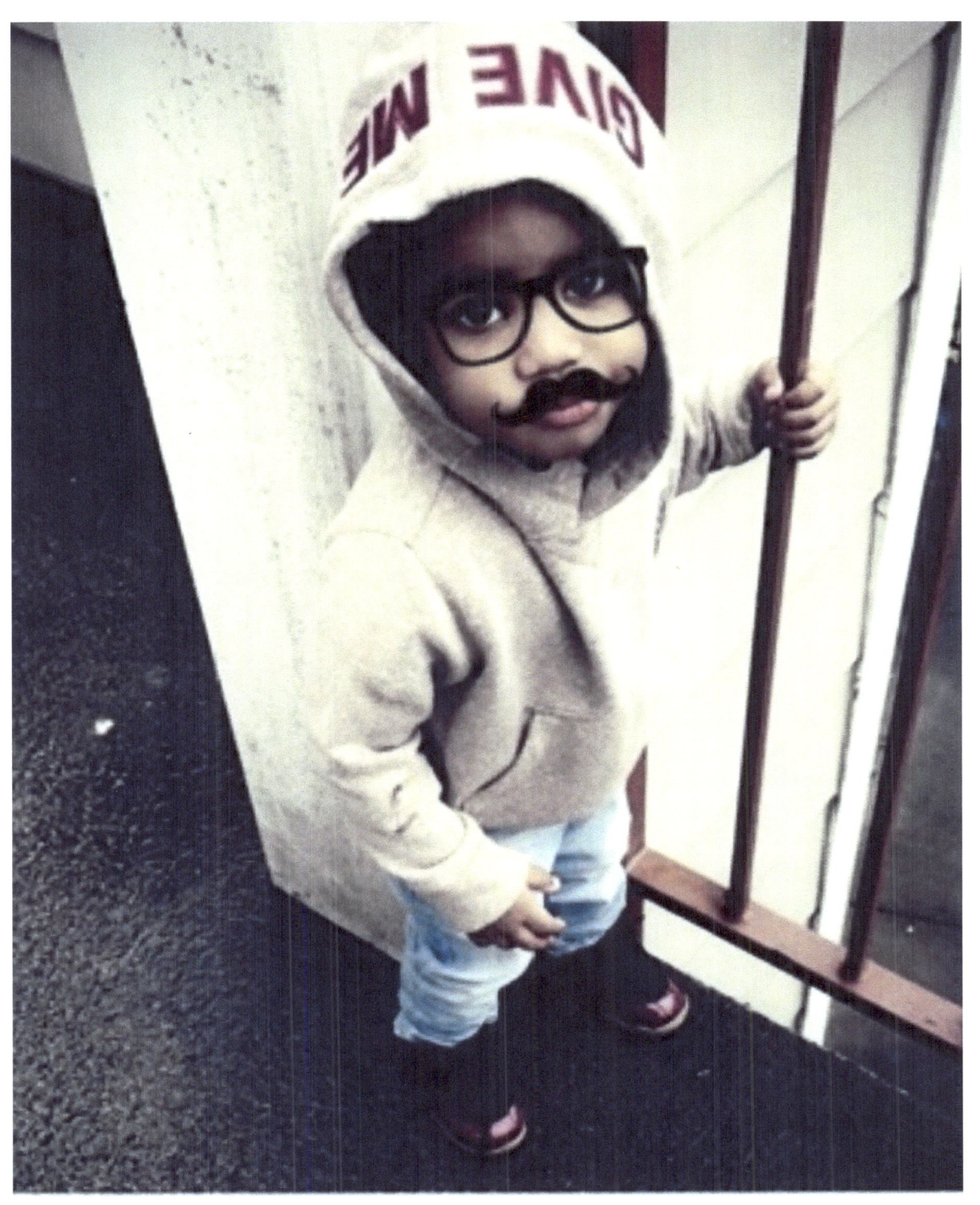

Mr Smarty pants

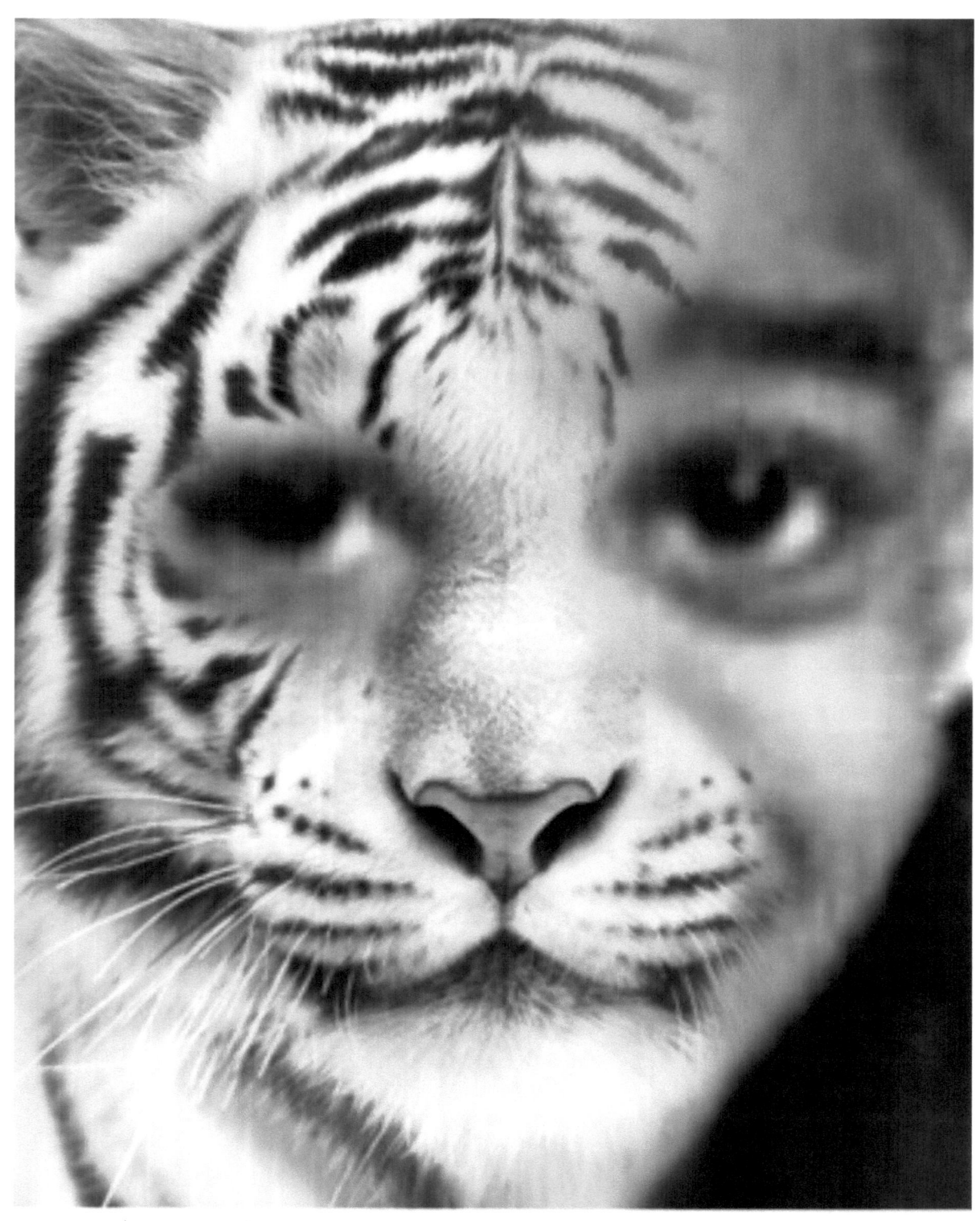

Raw

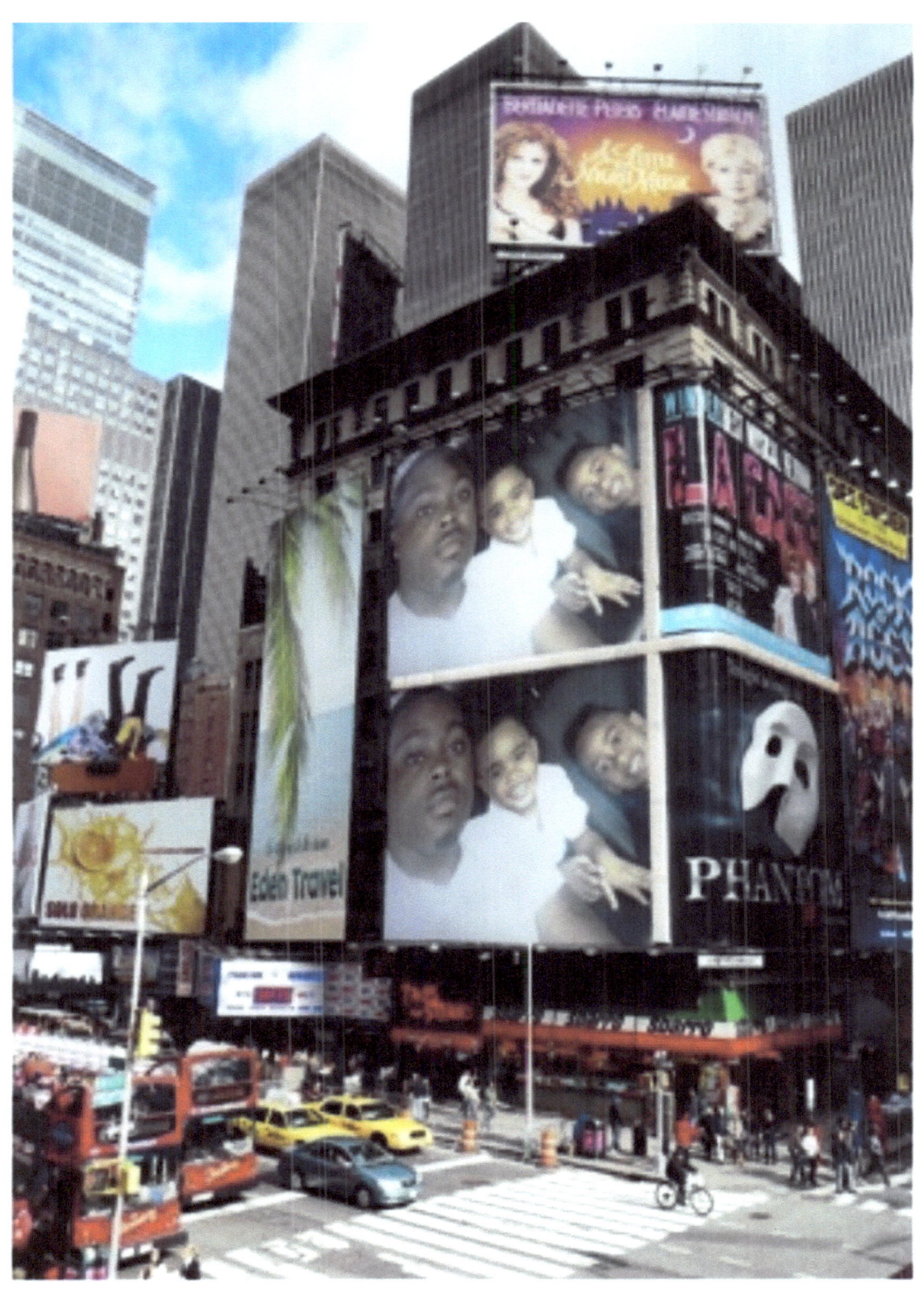

Billboard worthy for sure The Jackson's

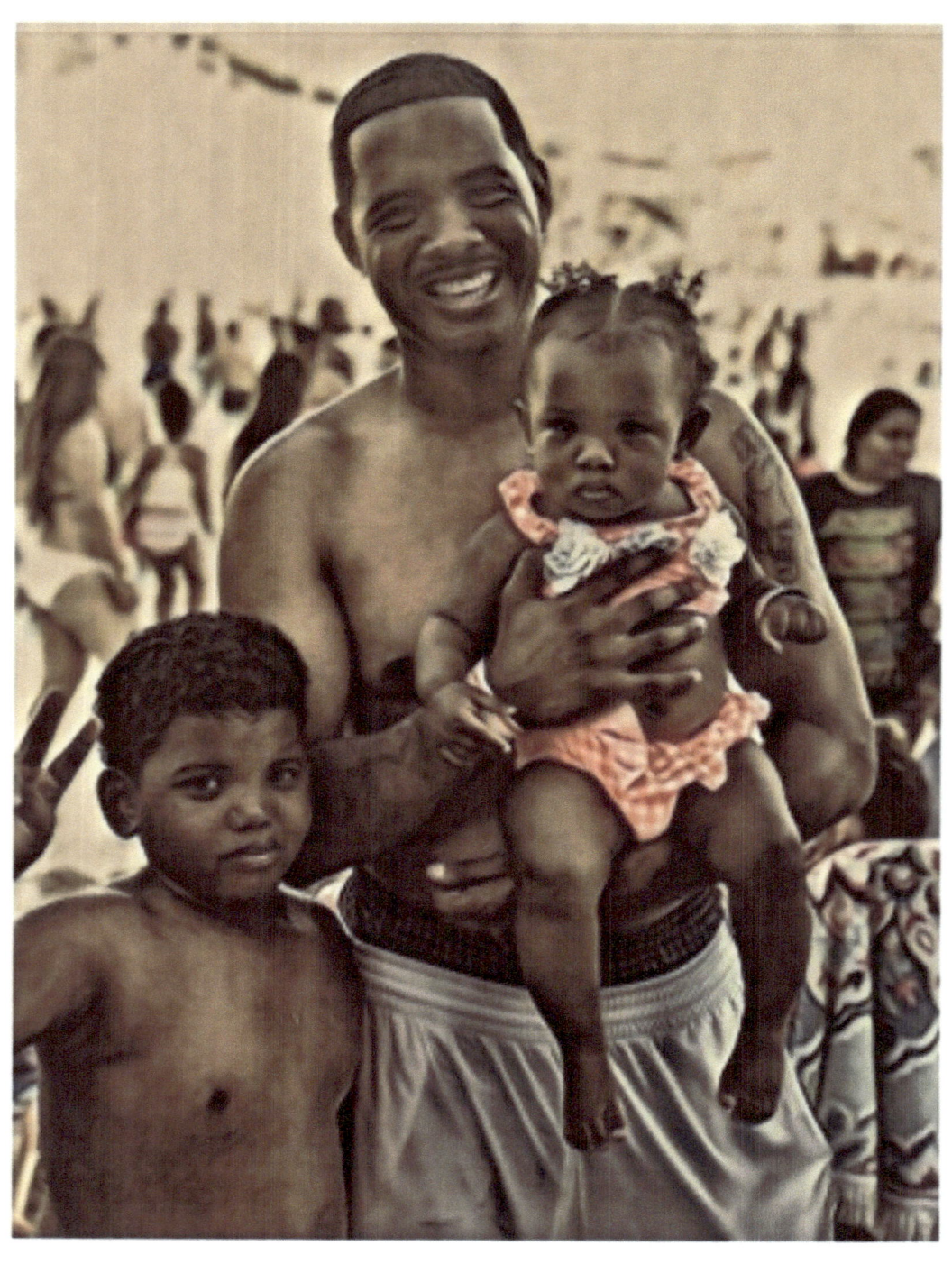

Daddy's boy and daddy's girl that's how it is with us Meet the Bauldwins

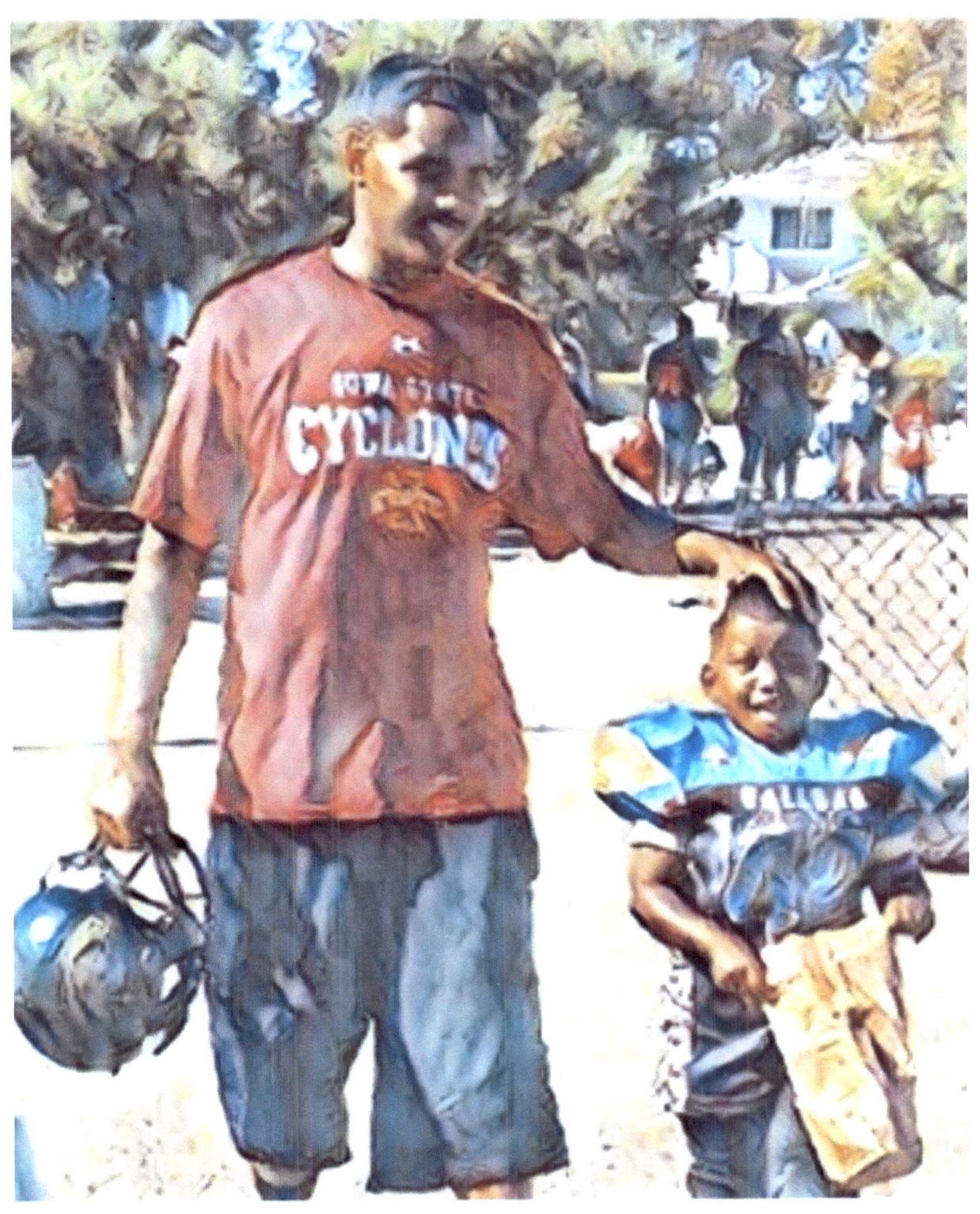

Good game son now let's go eat

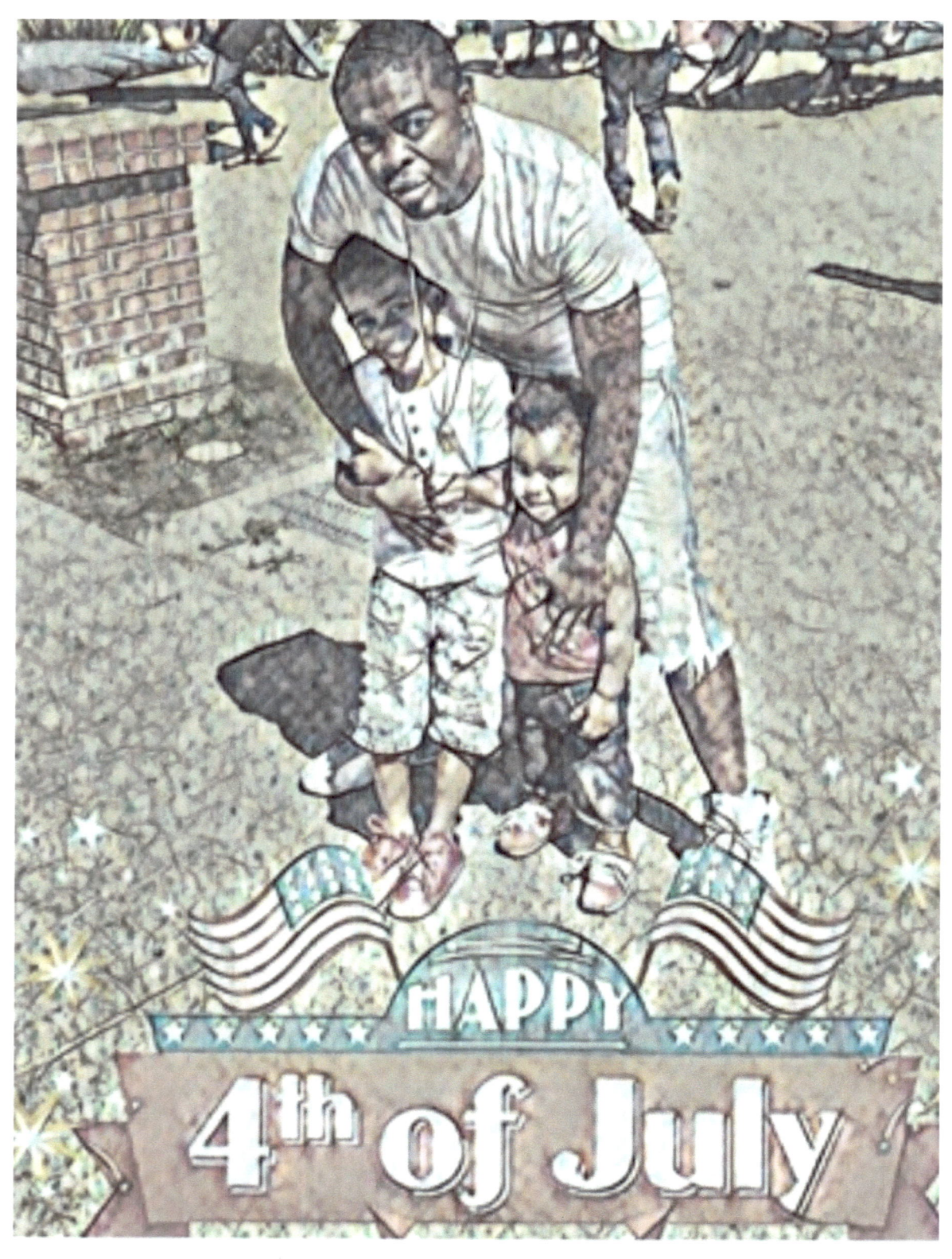

We love you all so much

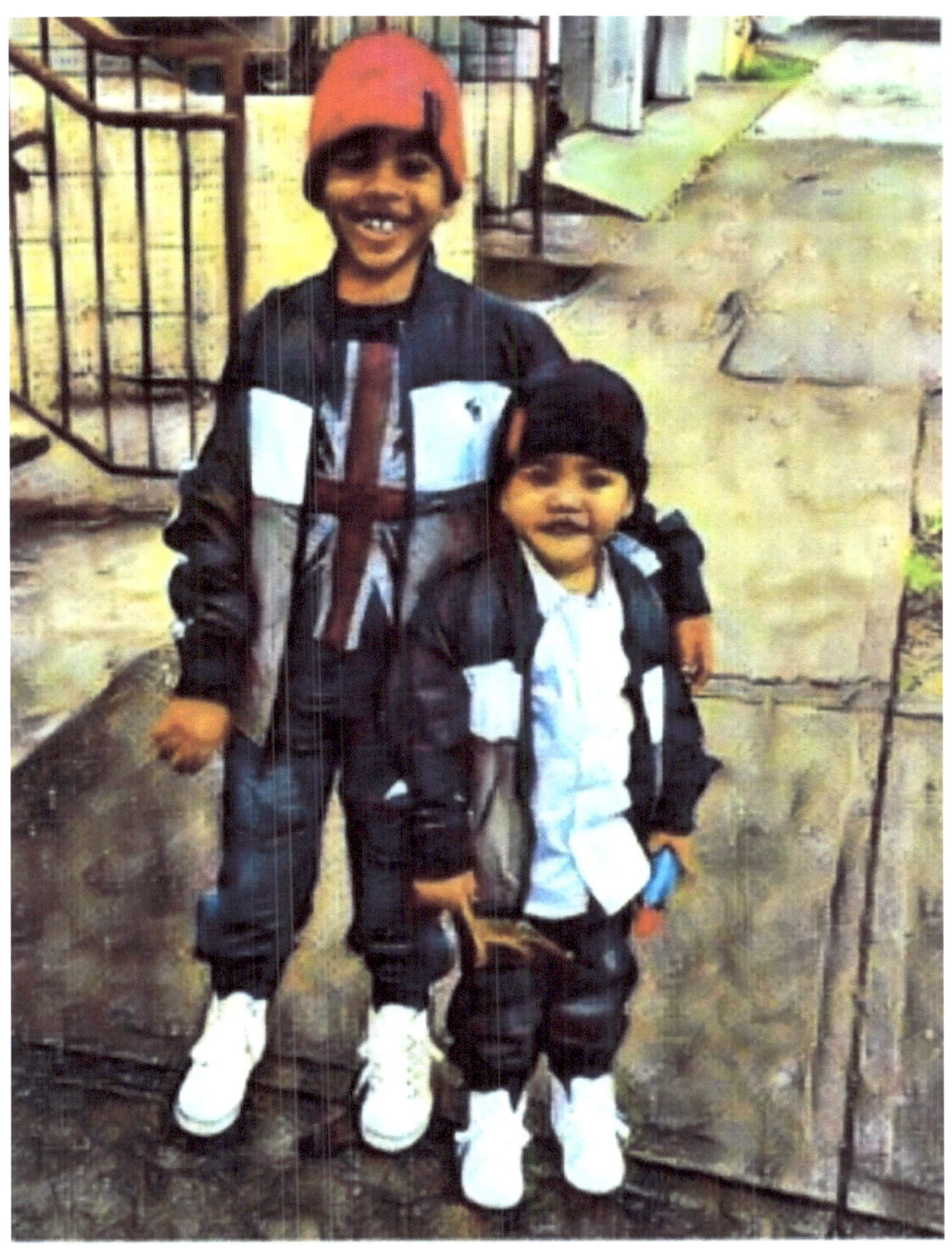

Brothers

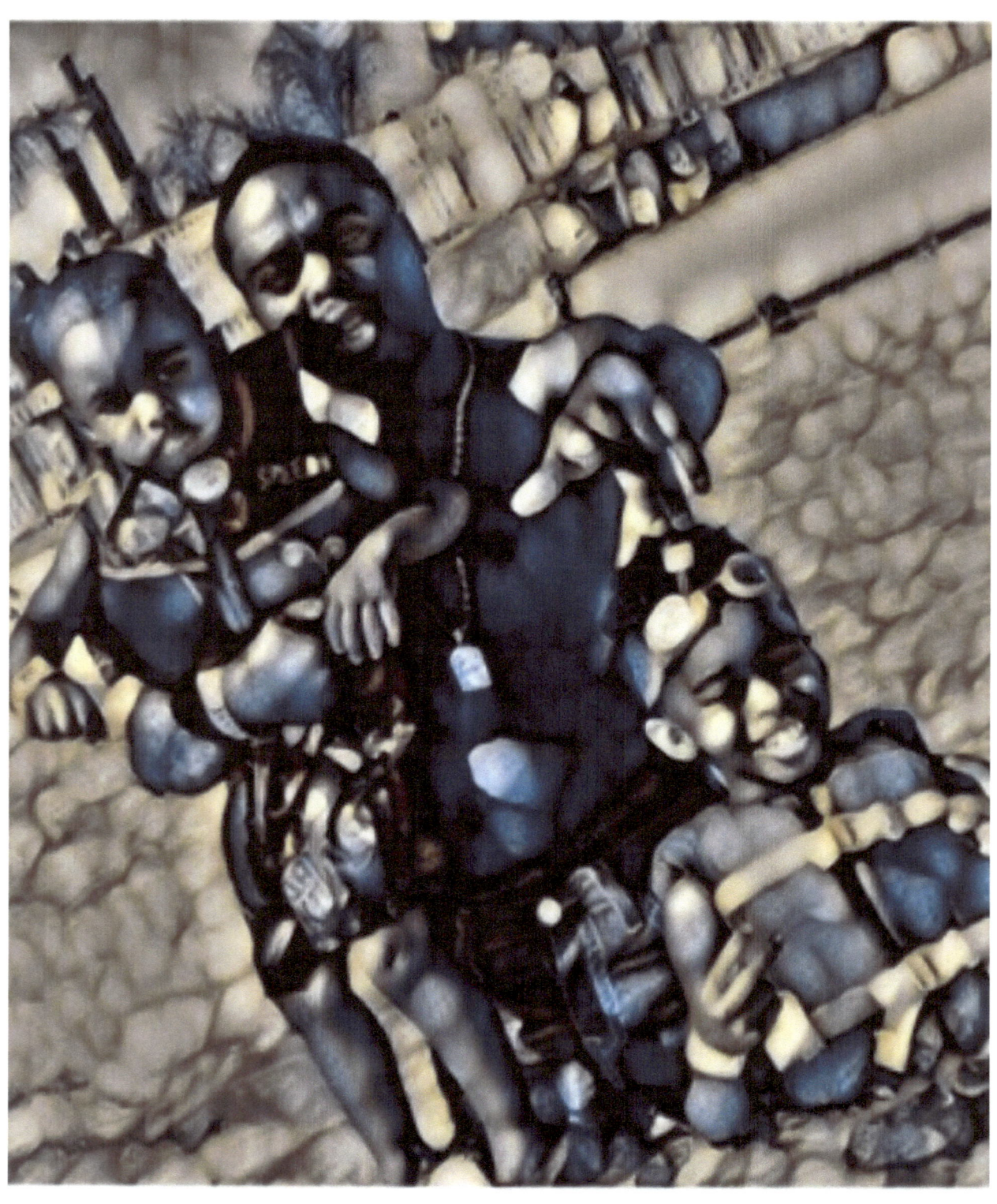

Daddy's our life saver

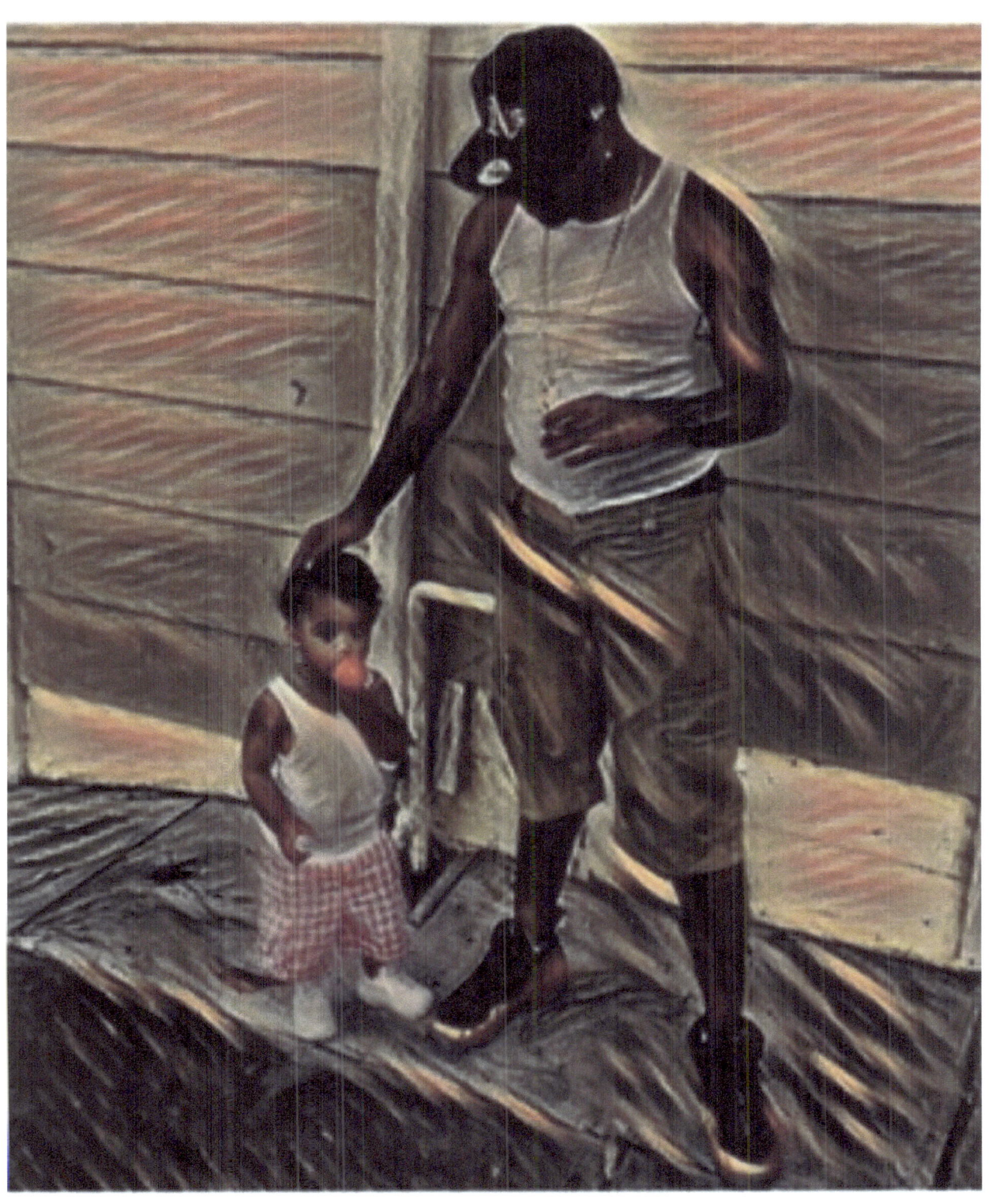

Listen kid Daddy loves you

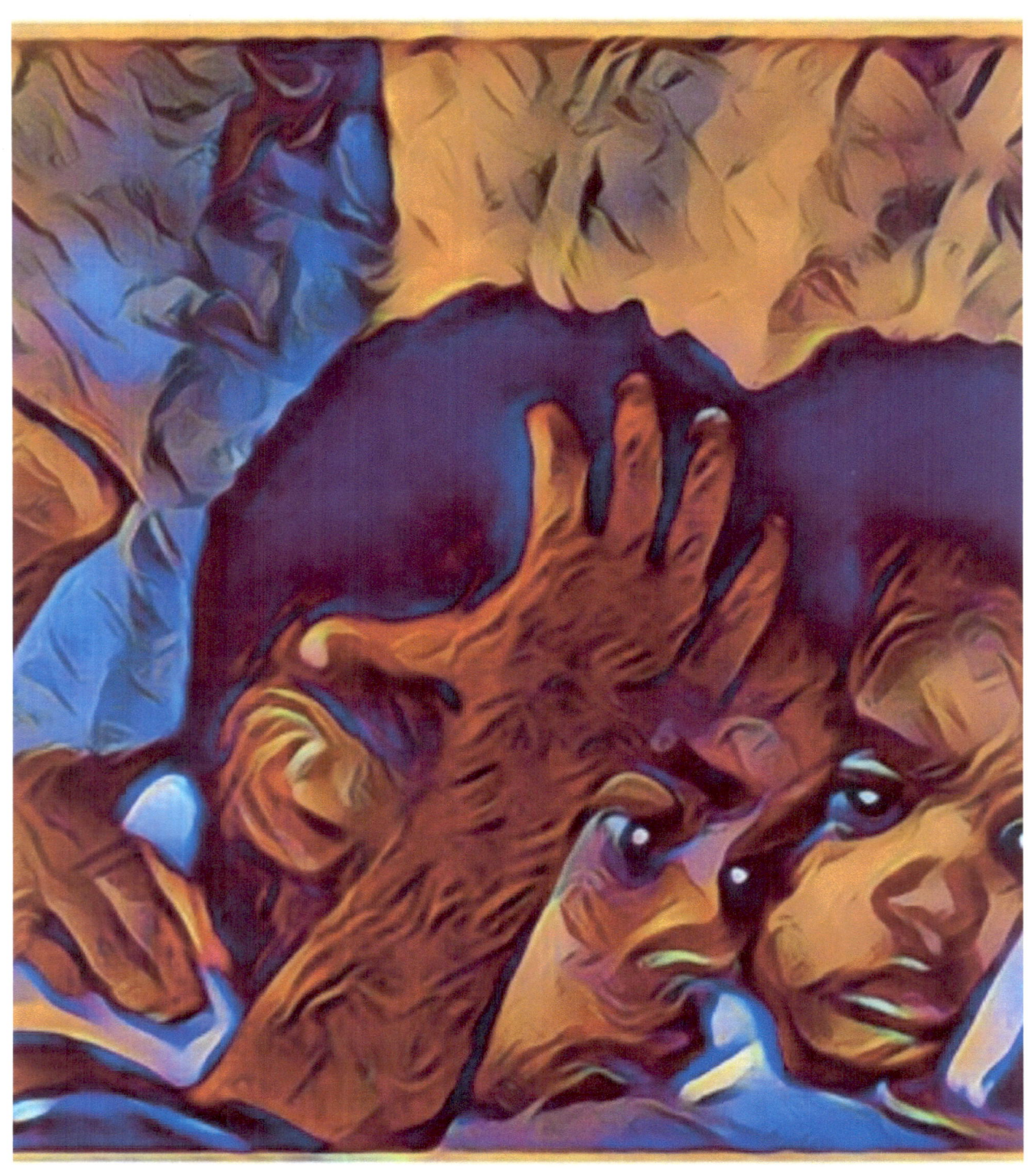

Unbreakable bond (brothers)

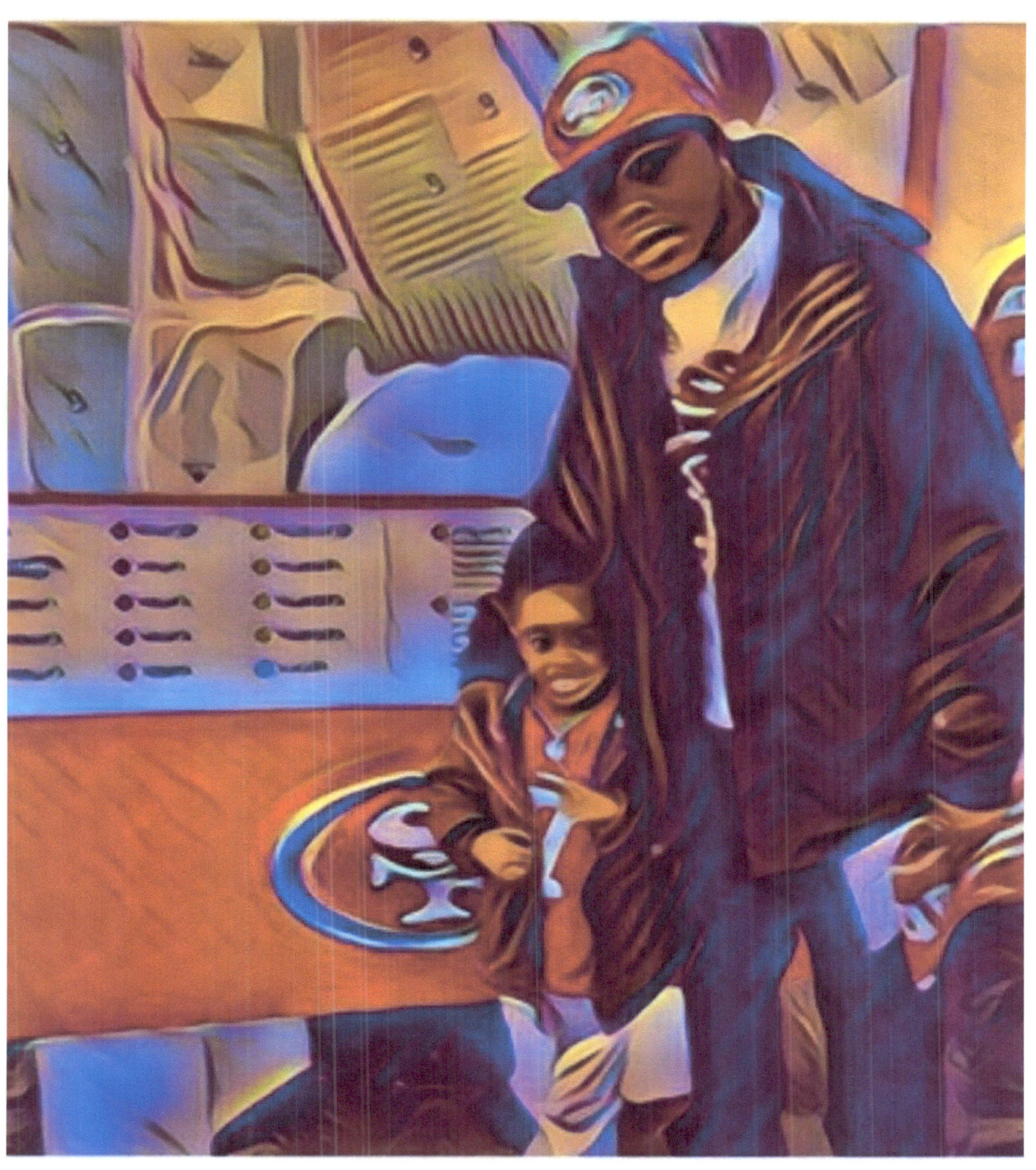

Fans of each other #fatherandson

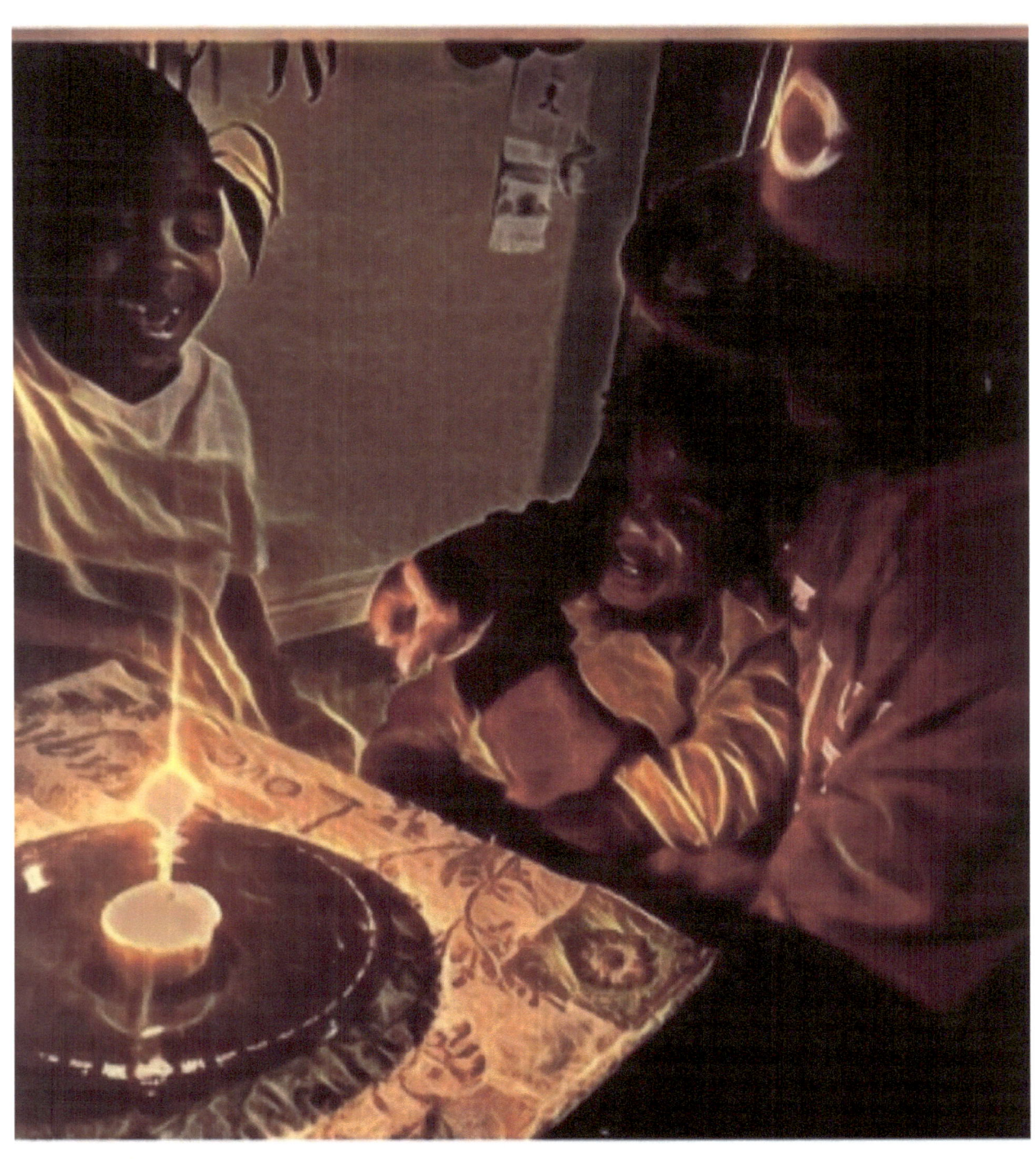

This picture sums us up literally #allsmiles

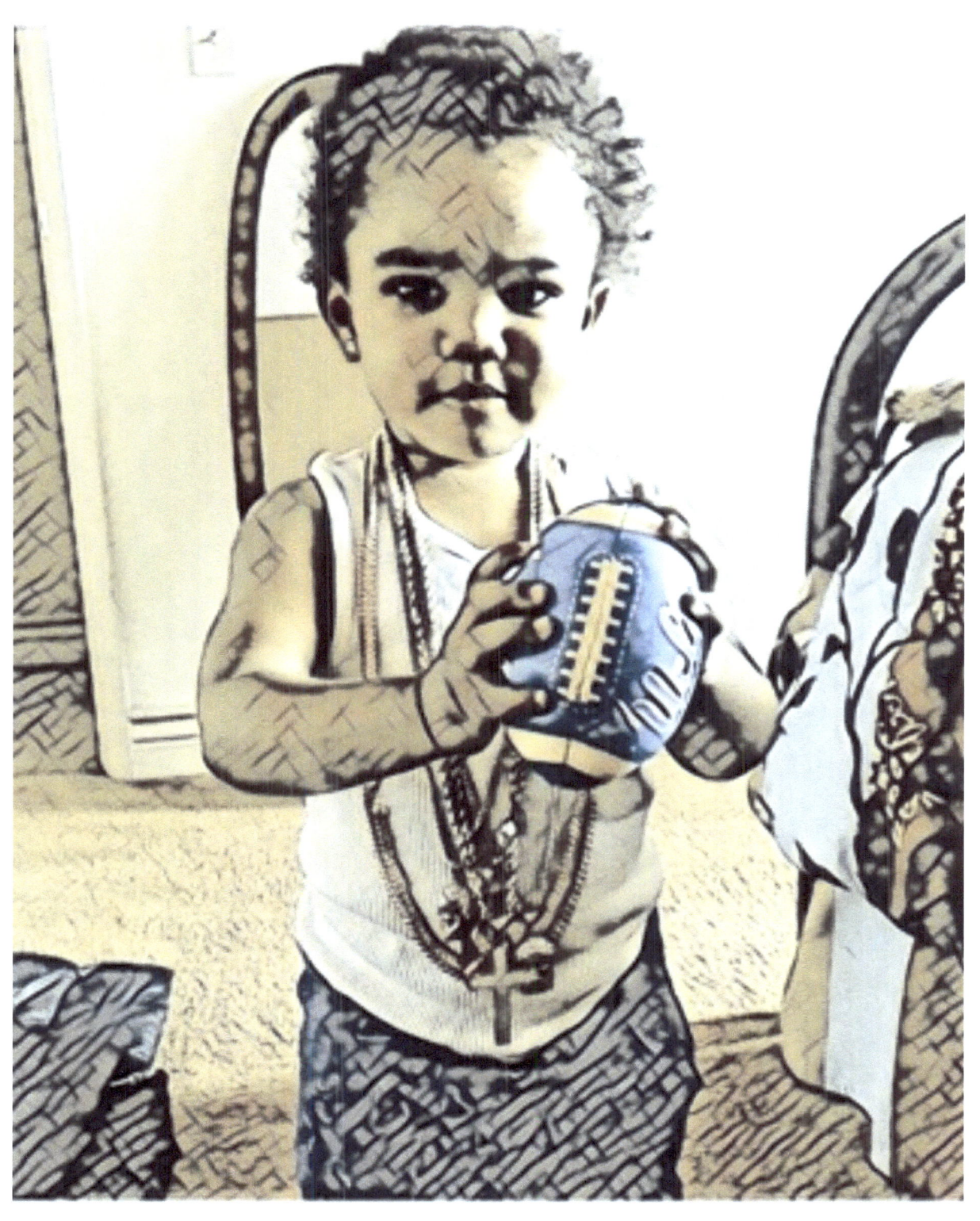

Mood always playtime

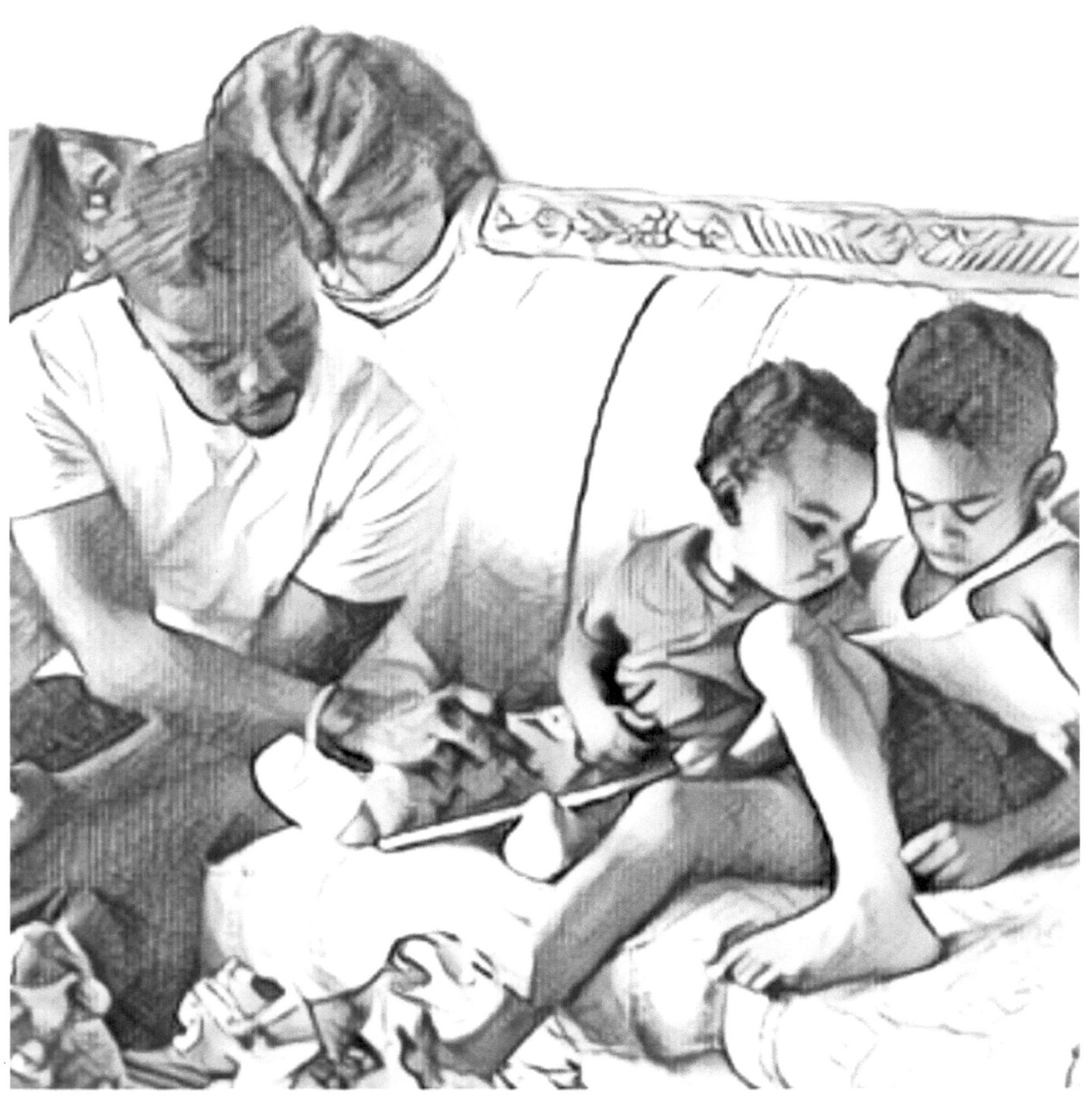

Love

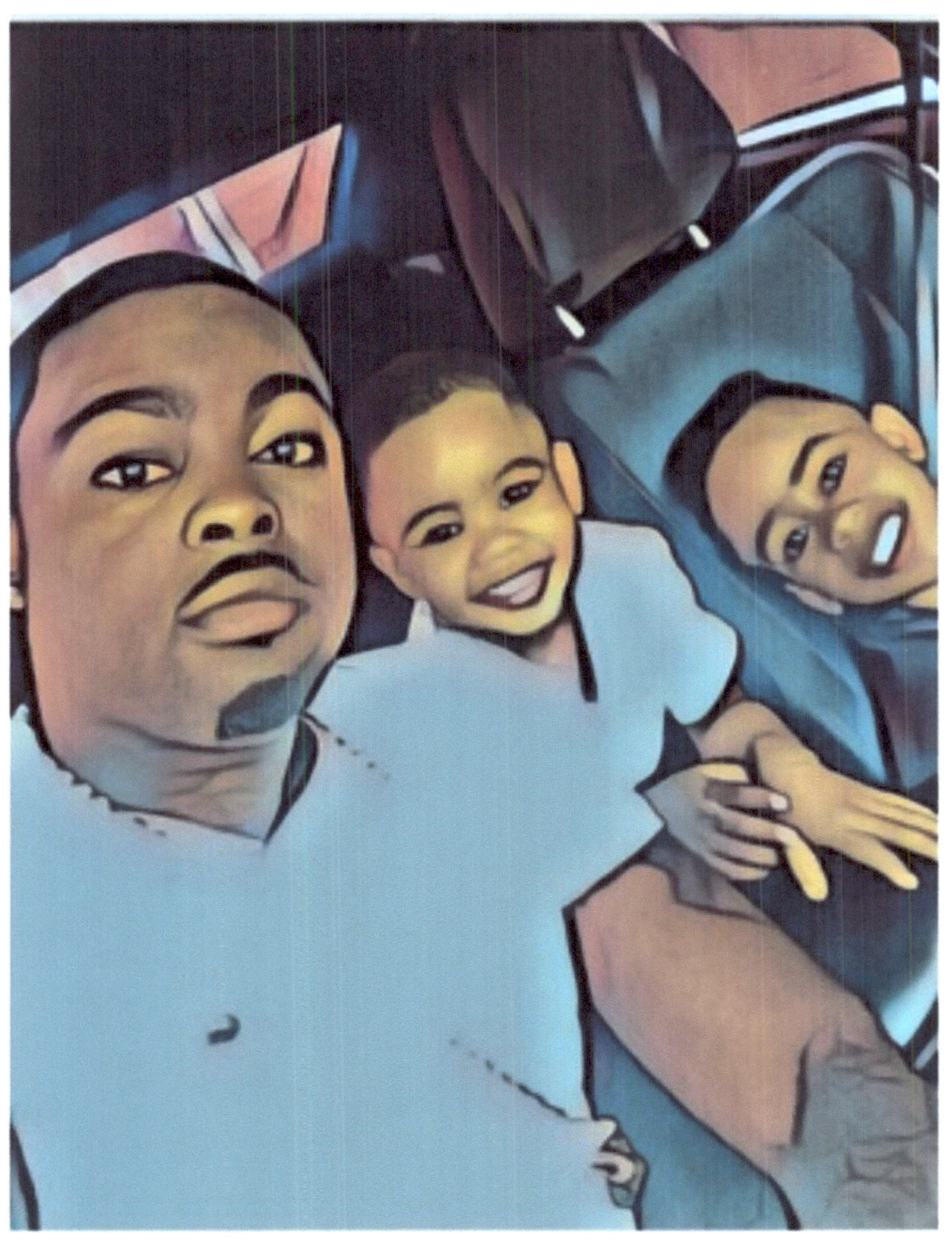

Us again

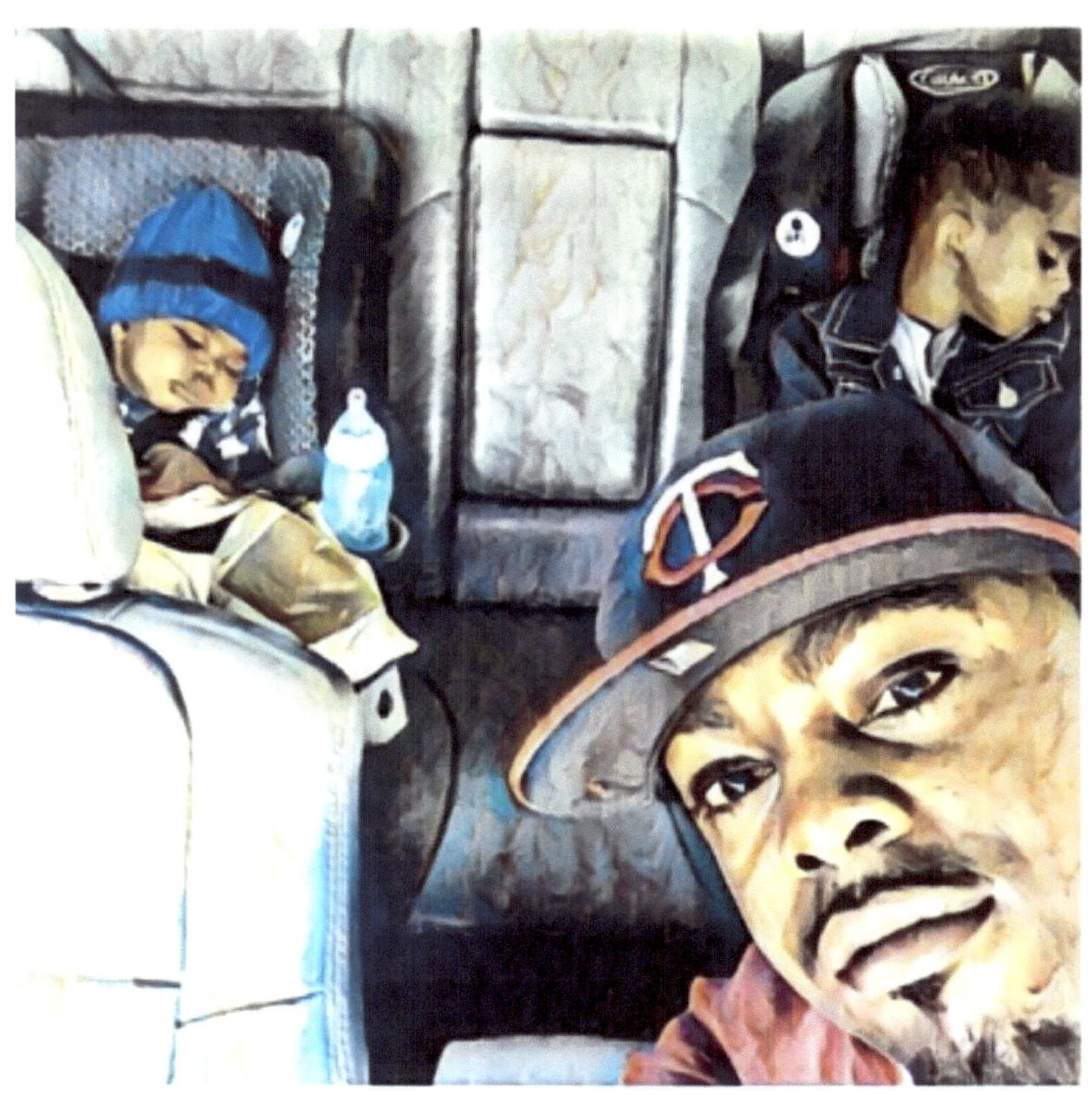

My reasons why

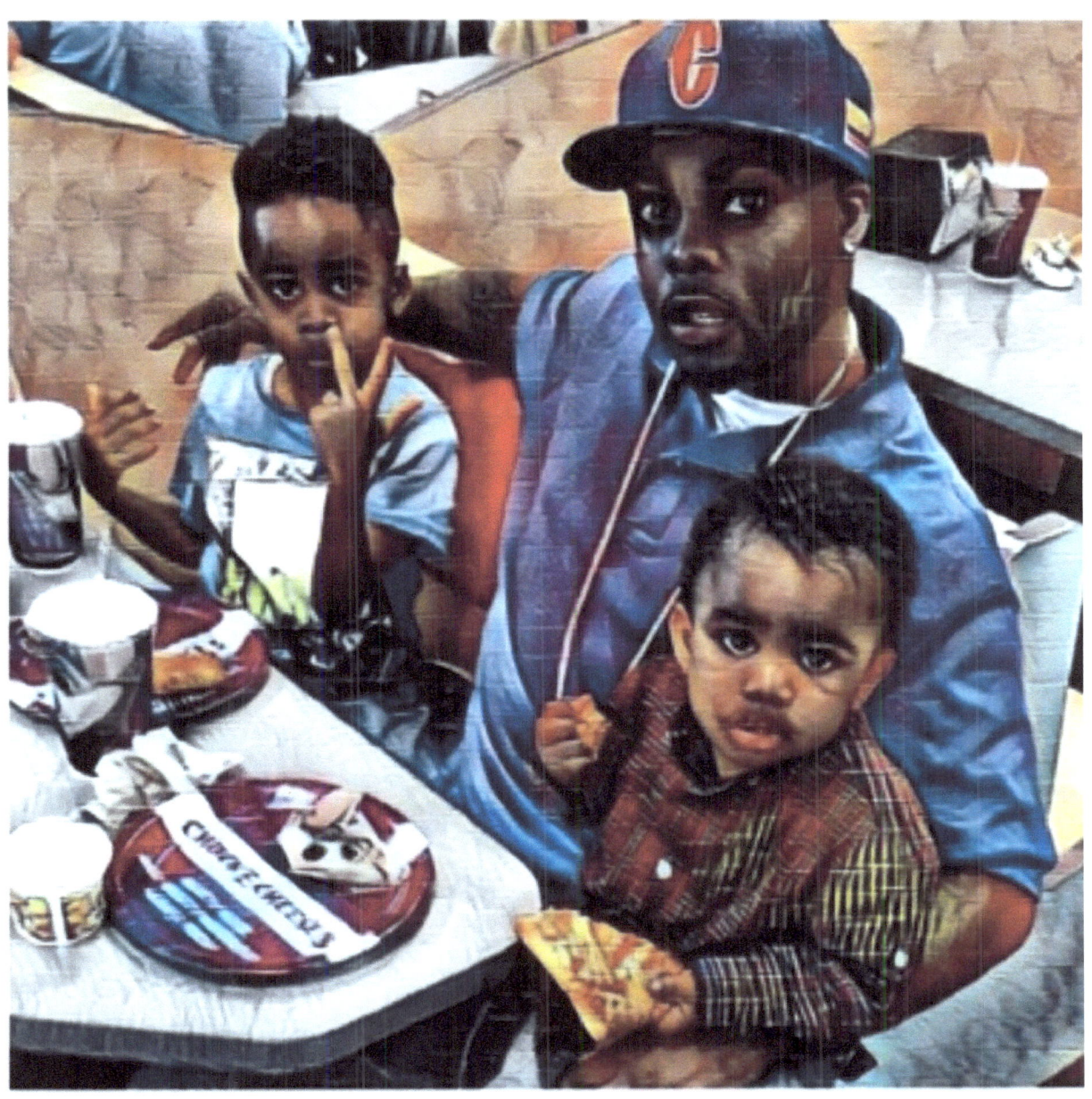

Can you guess where we're at? The coolest place in the world

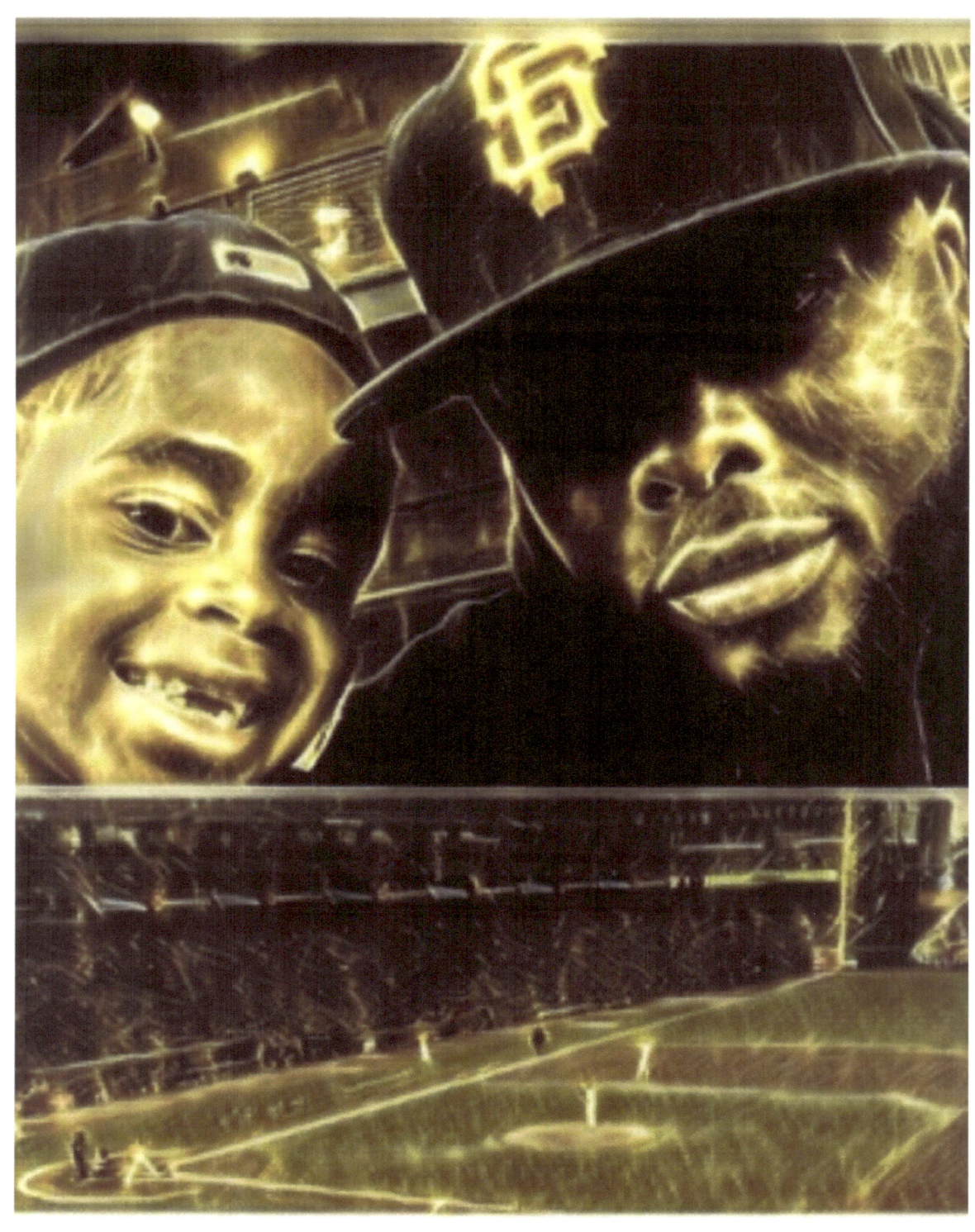

We're each other's support system

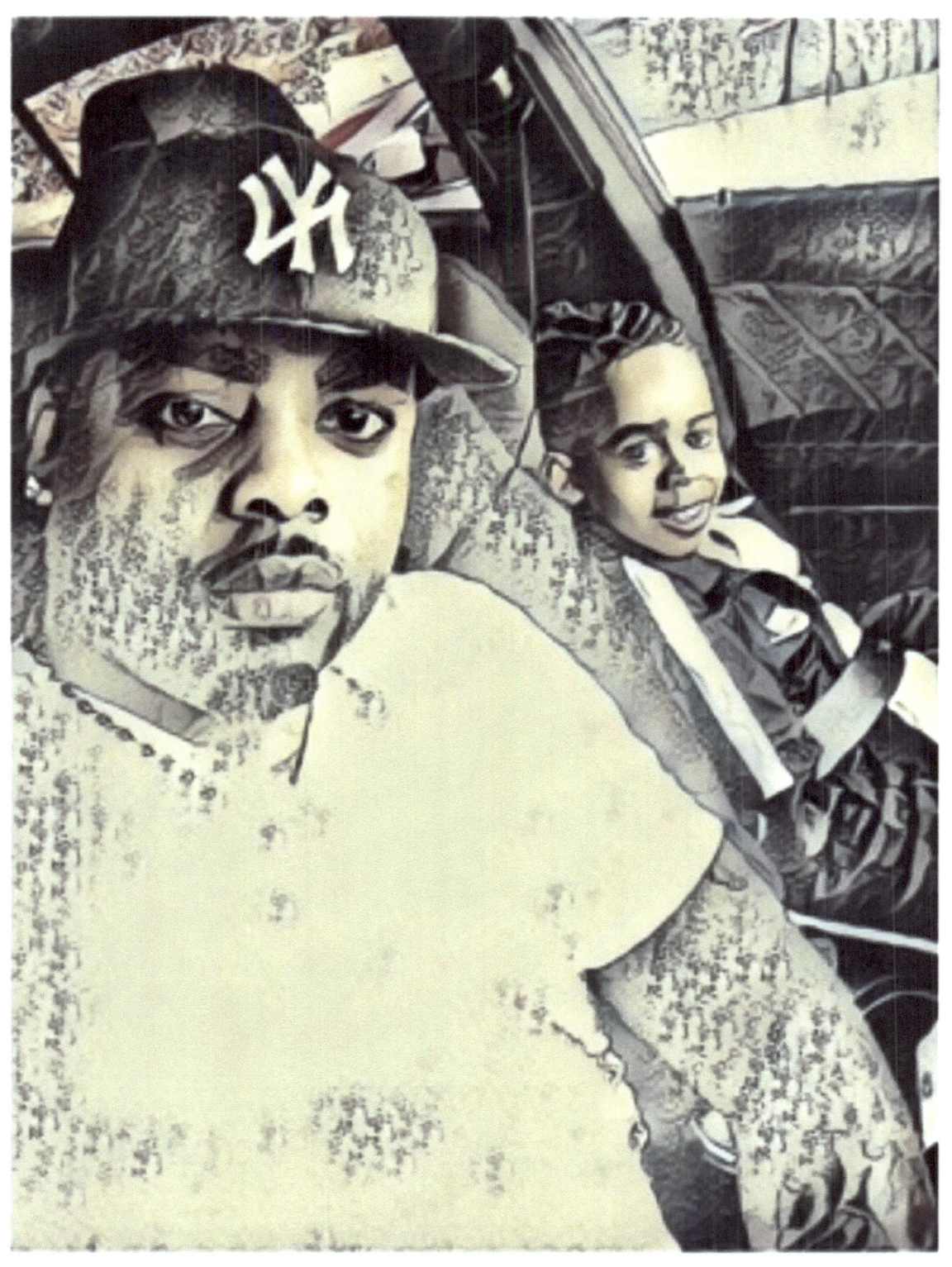

Oh hey world

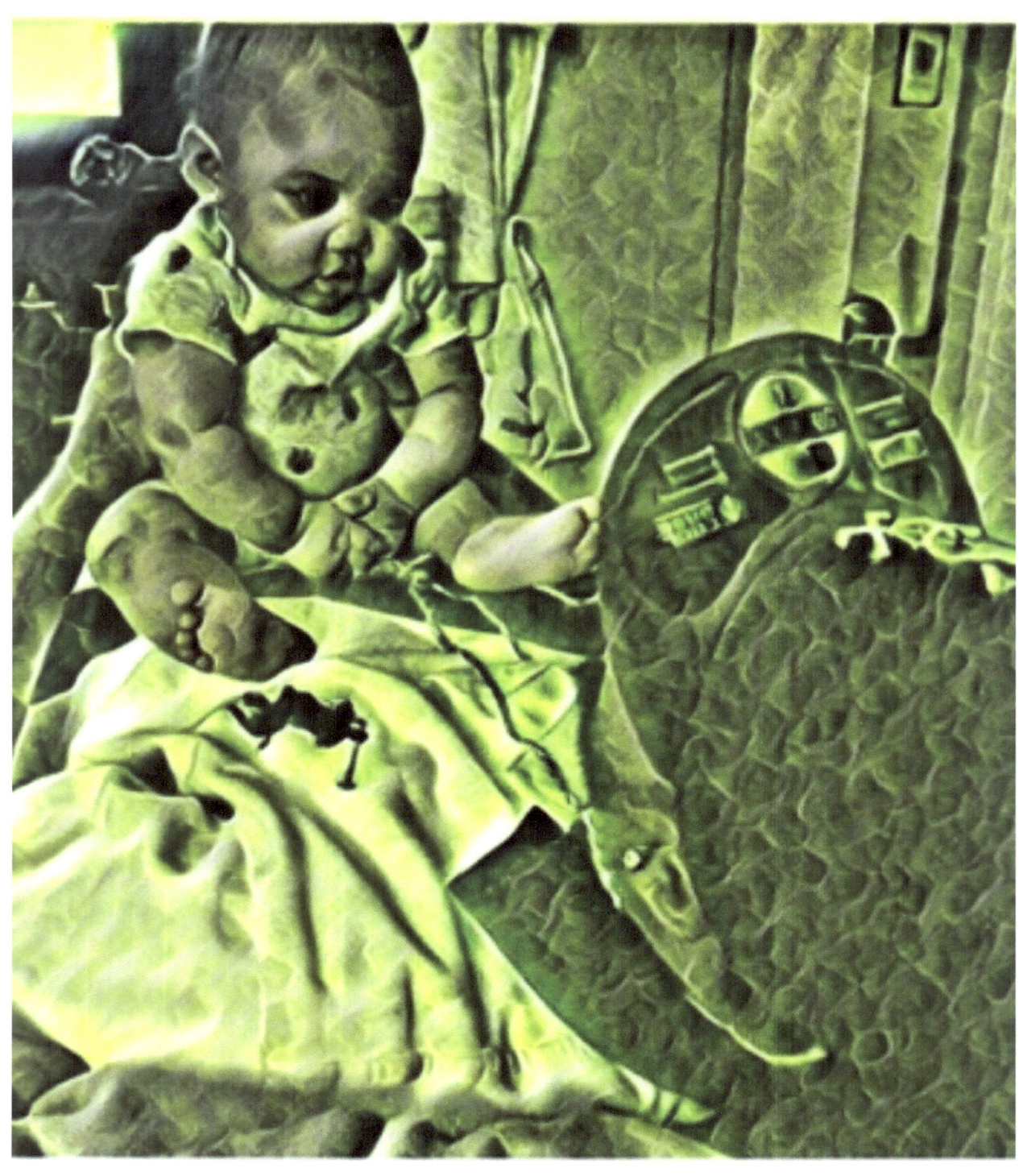

I love you unconditionally son you'll understand one day

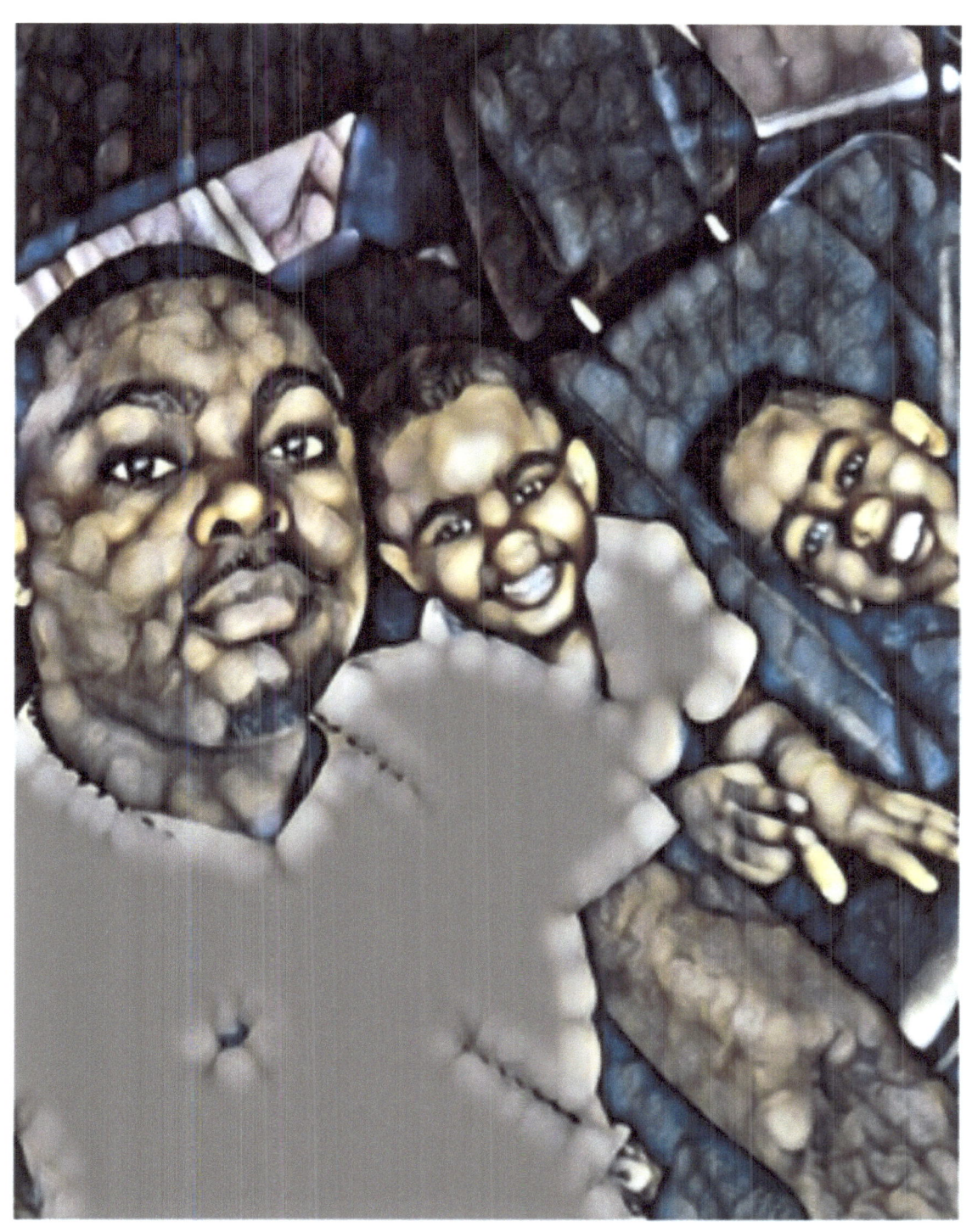

We're the Jackson's

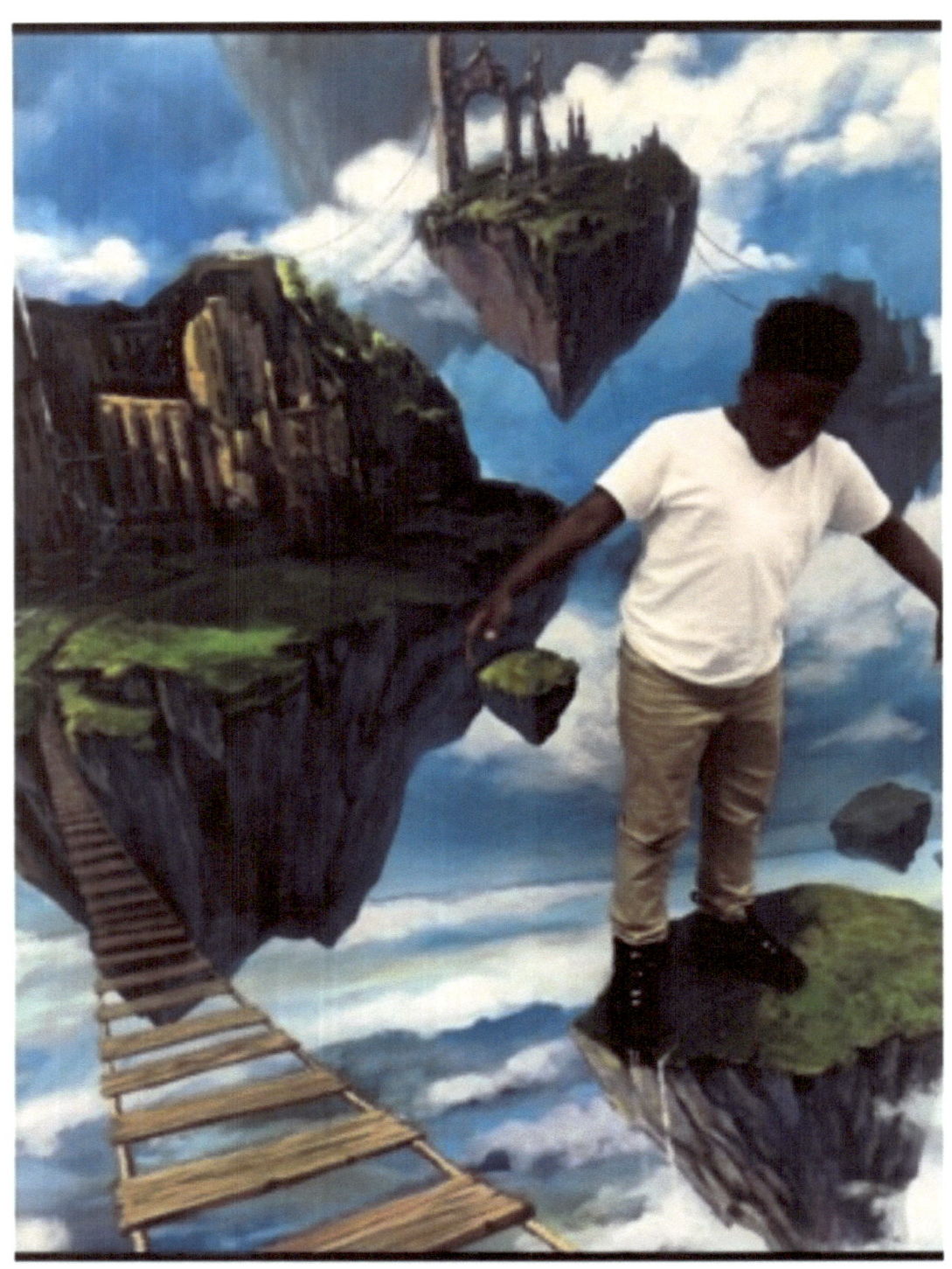

Nothing going to stop me from getting to the top

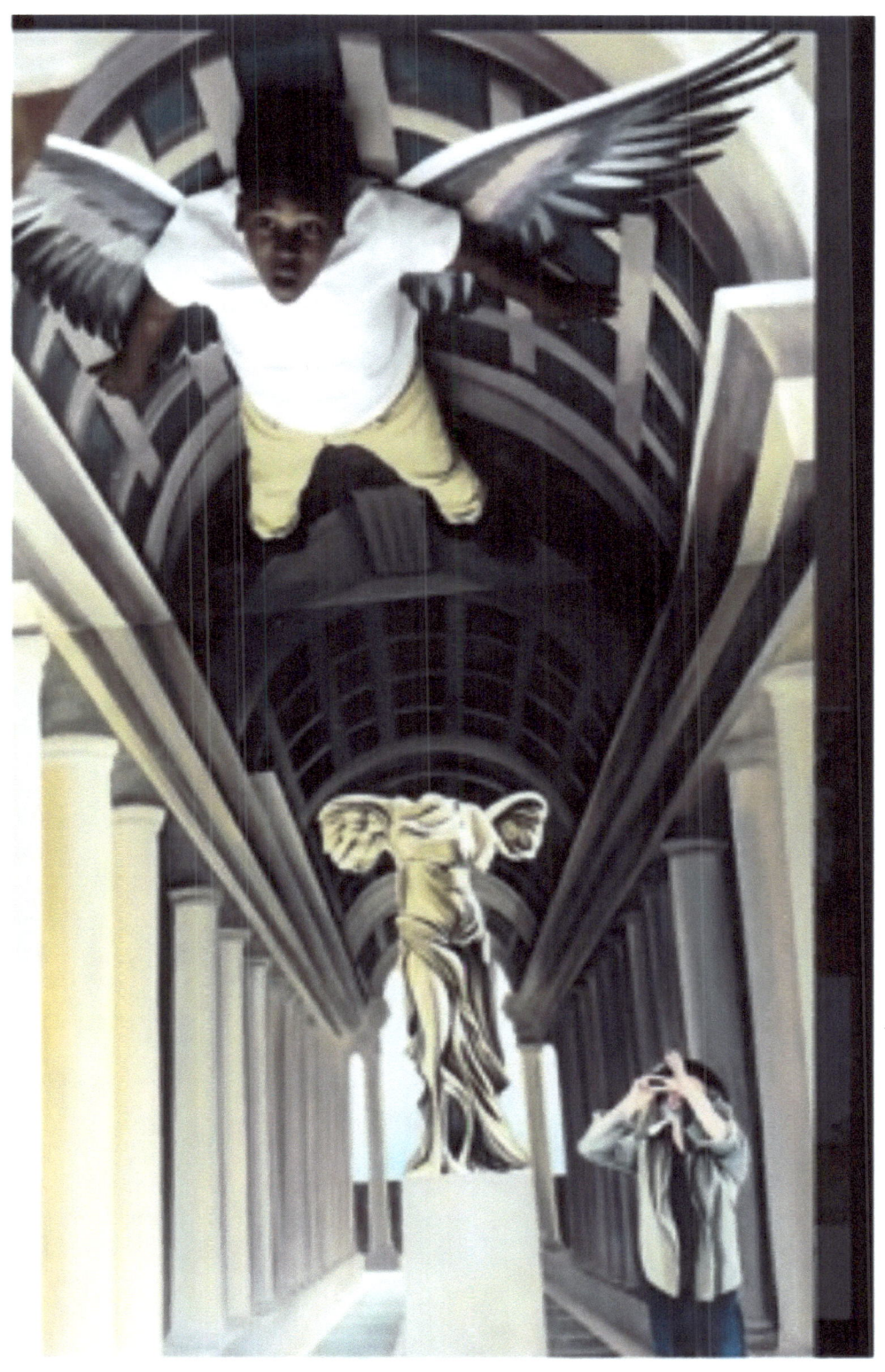

Highly blessed and favored

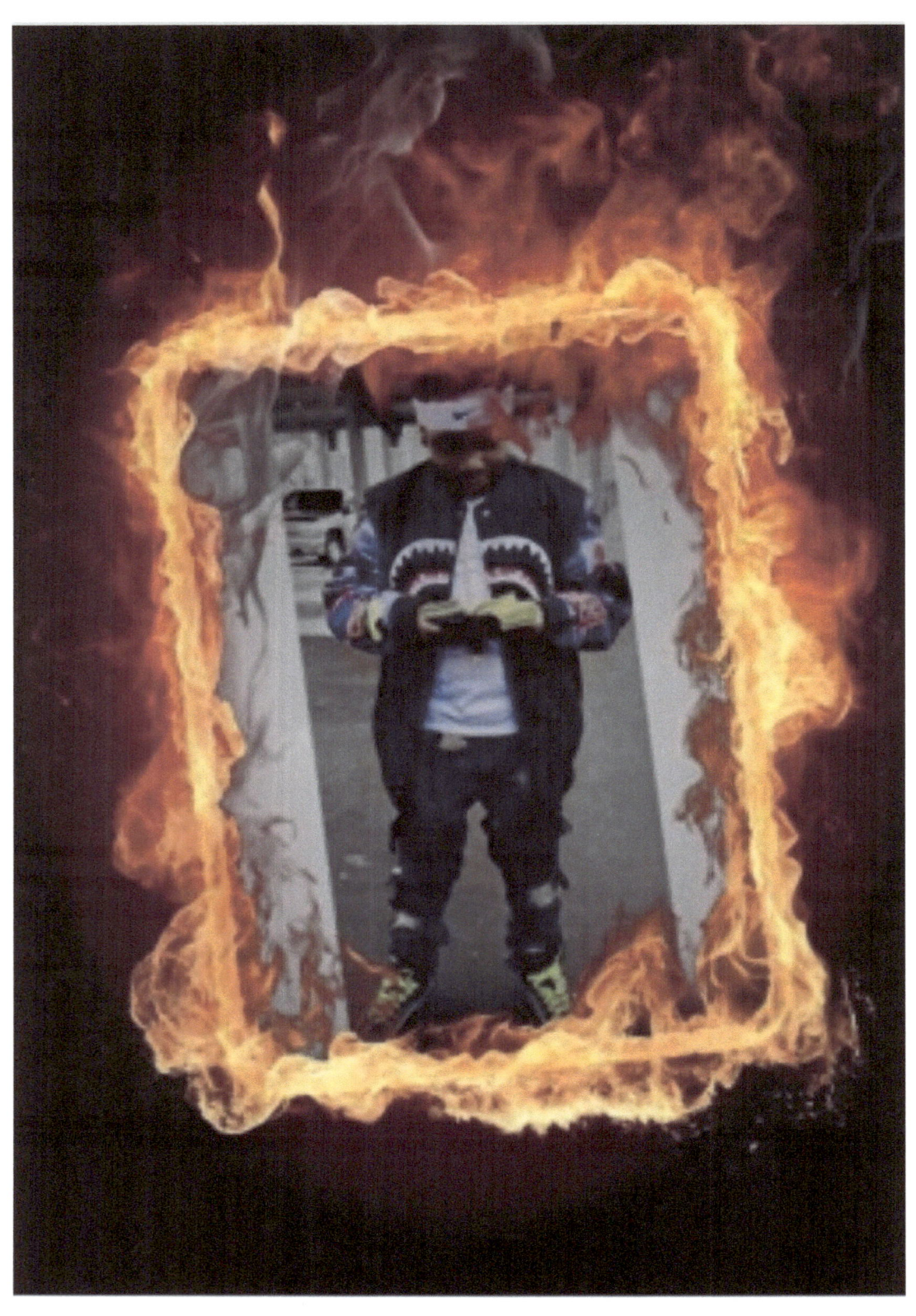

Yeah yeah I know I'm on fire

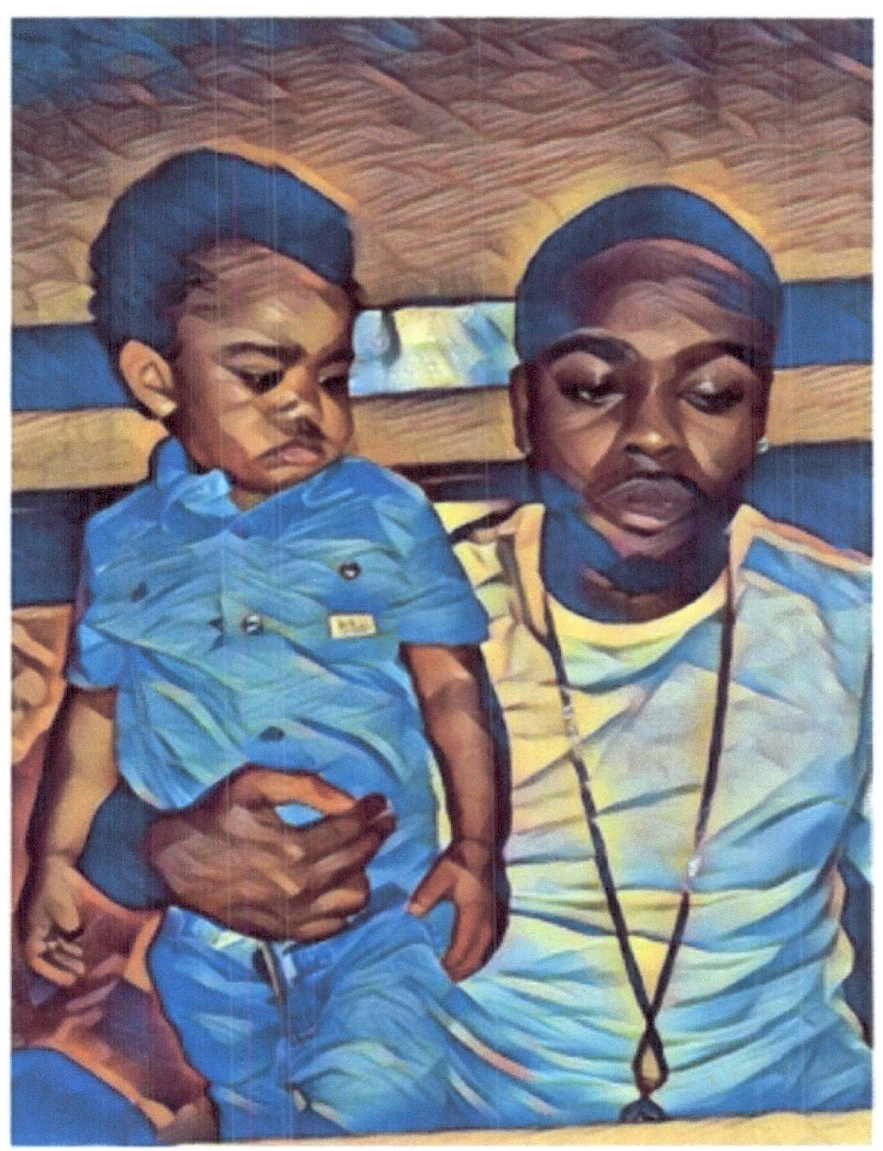

Dylan: what's that dad? Daddy: I don't know son but we ain't eating it

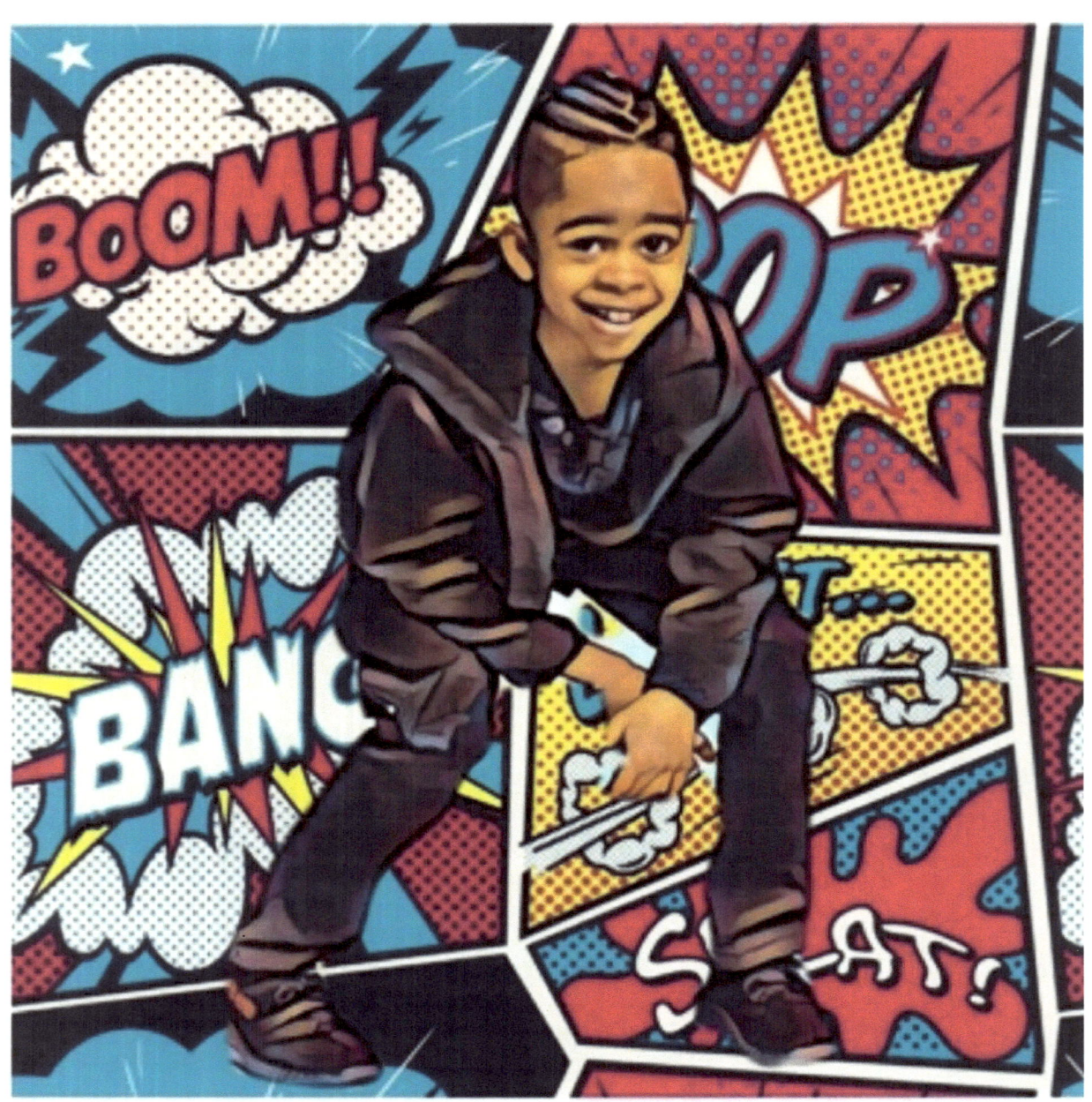

Bam !!

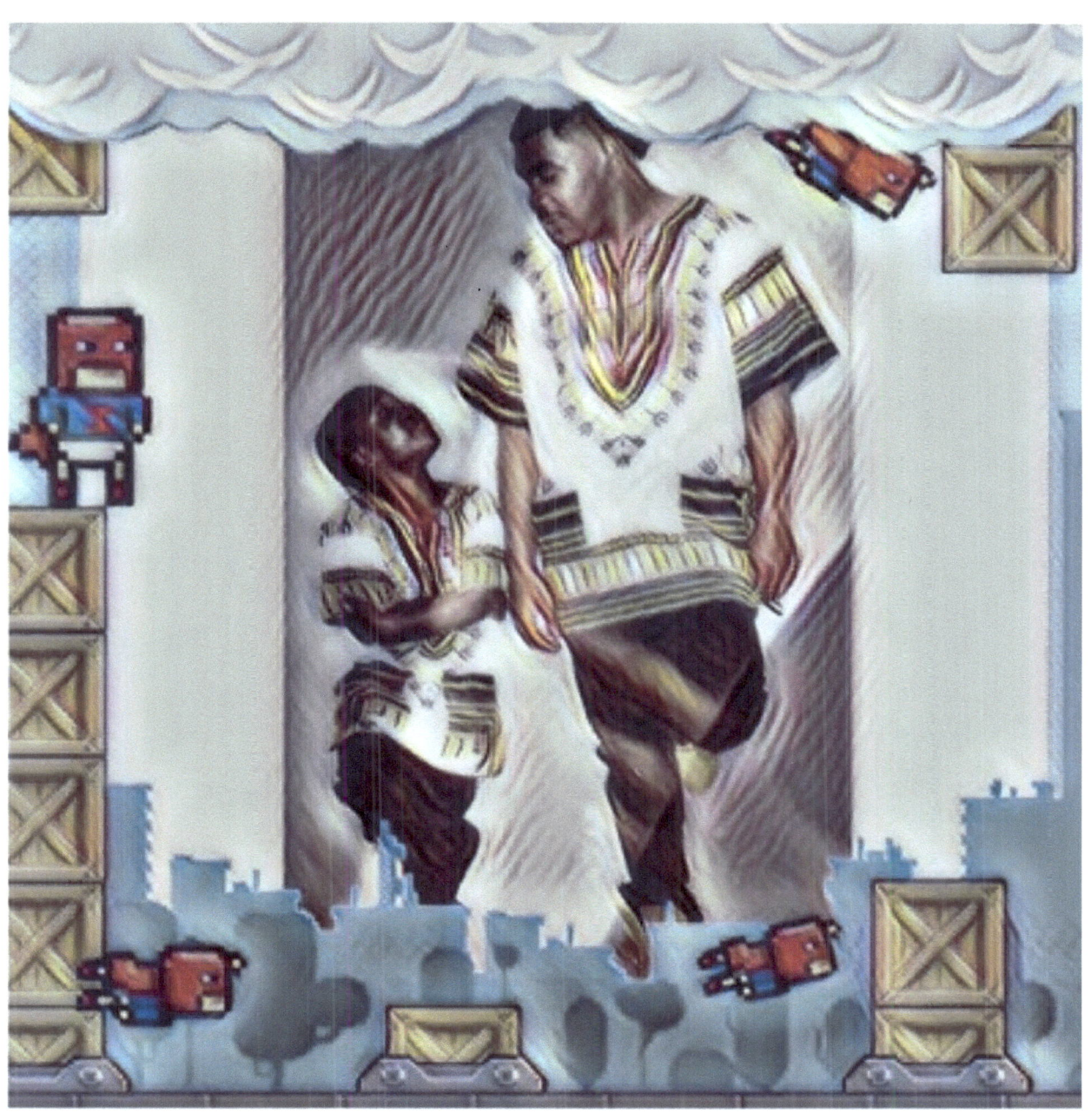

I love you daddy

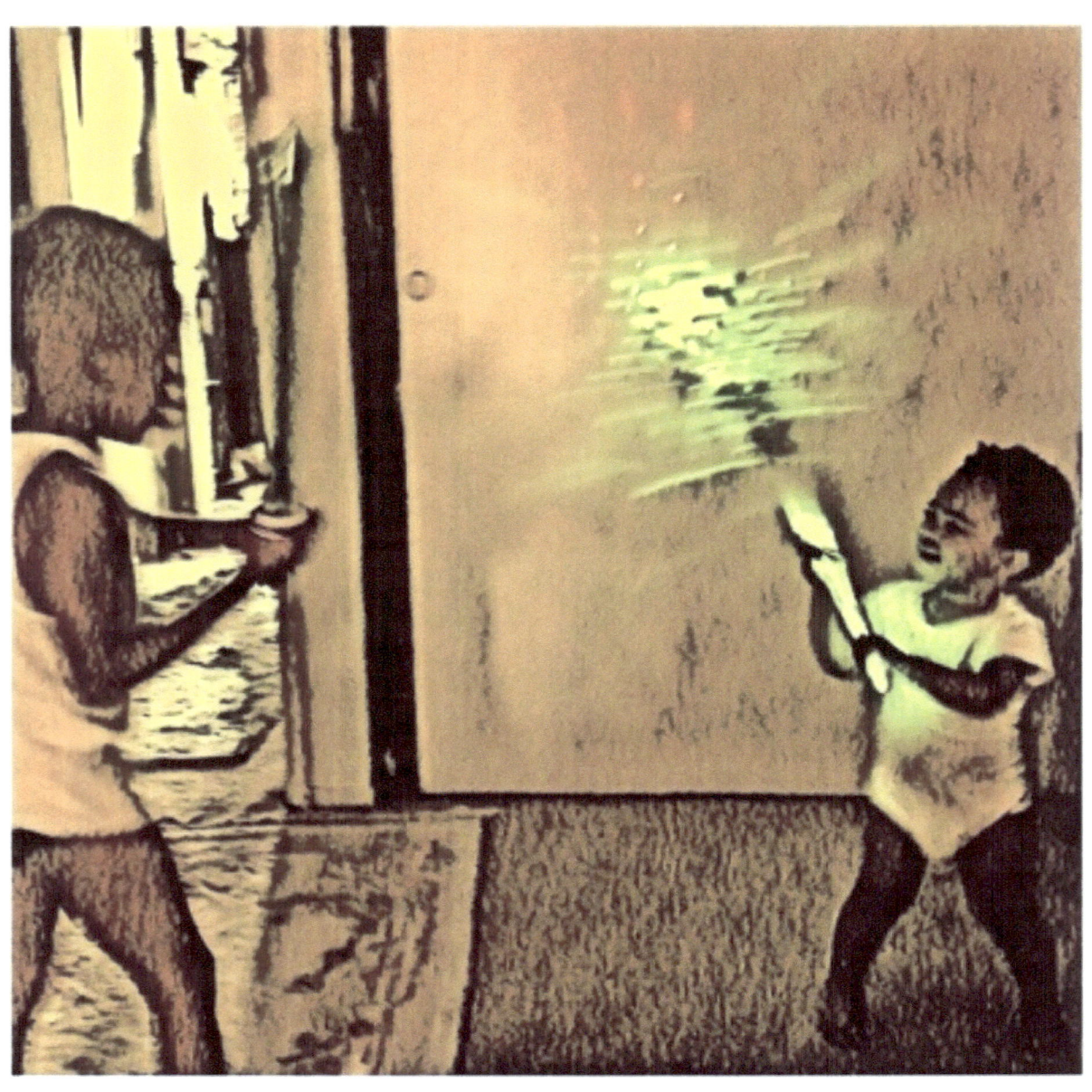

You want a piece of me ?

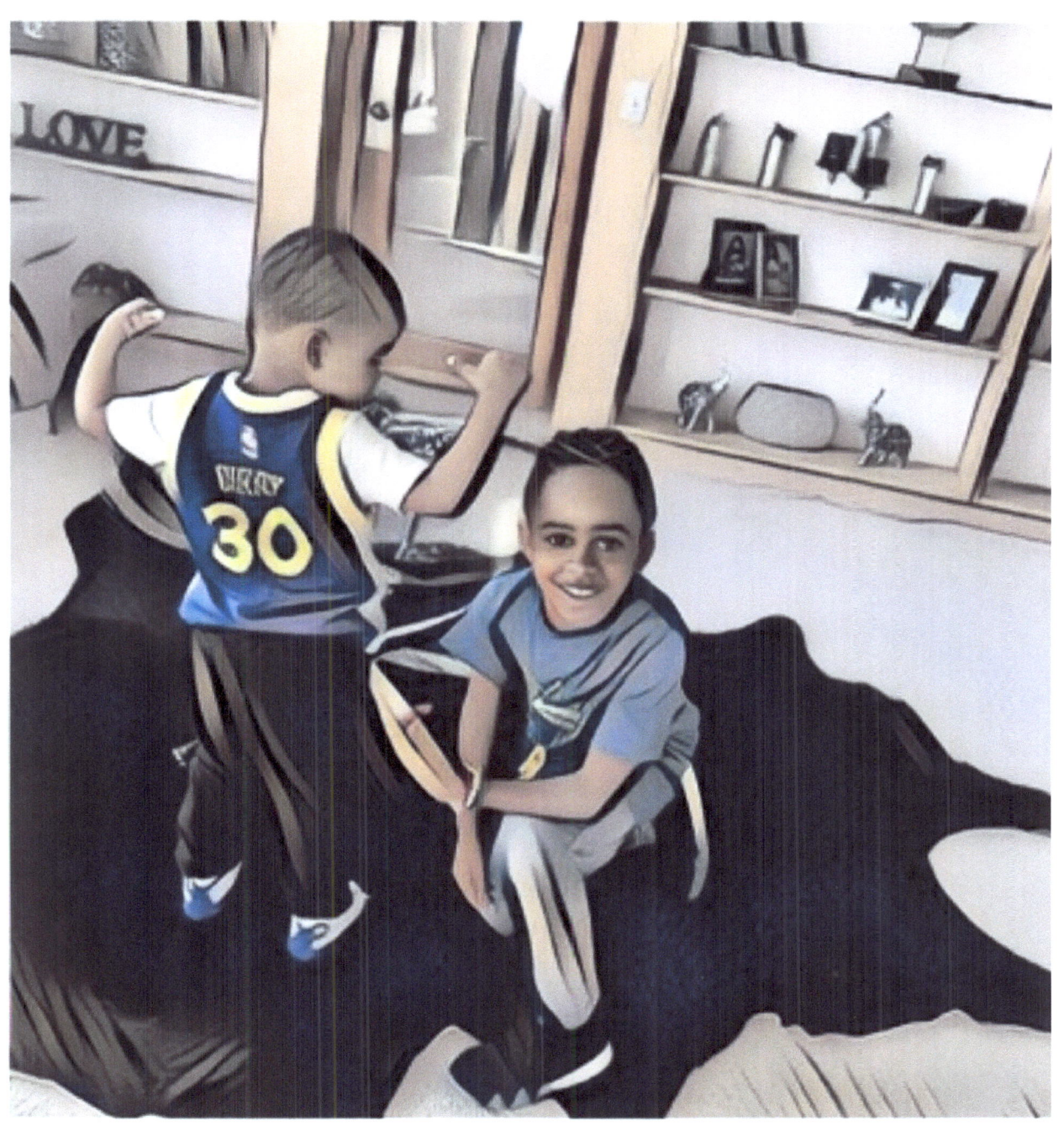

All Day Everyday Warriors

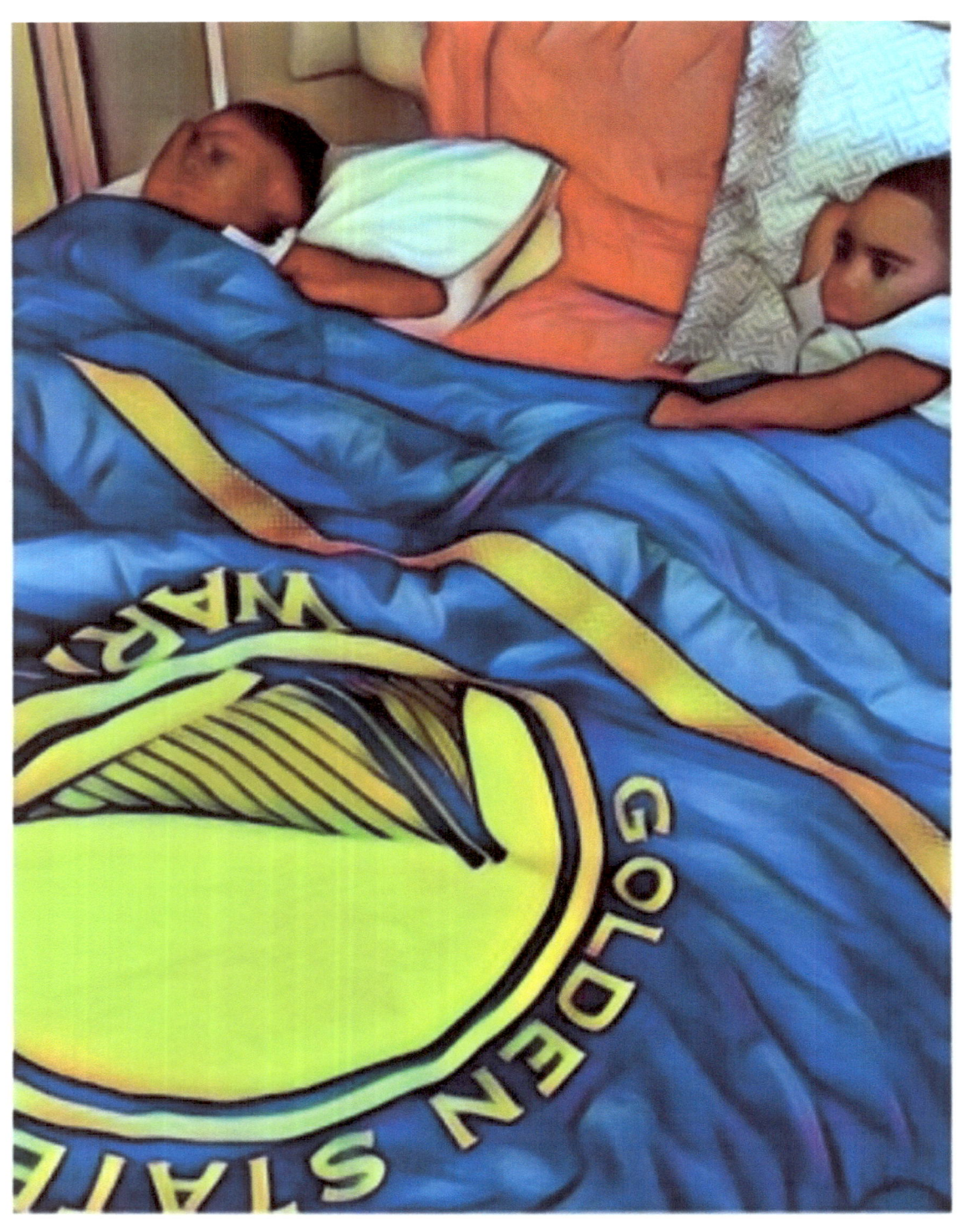

Warriors Baby

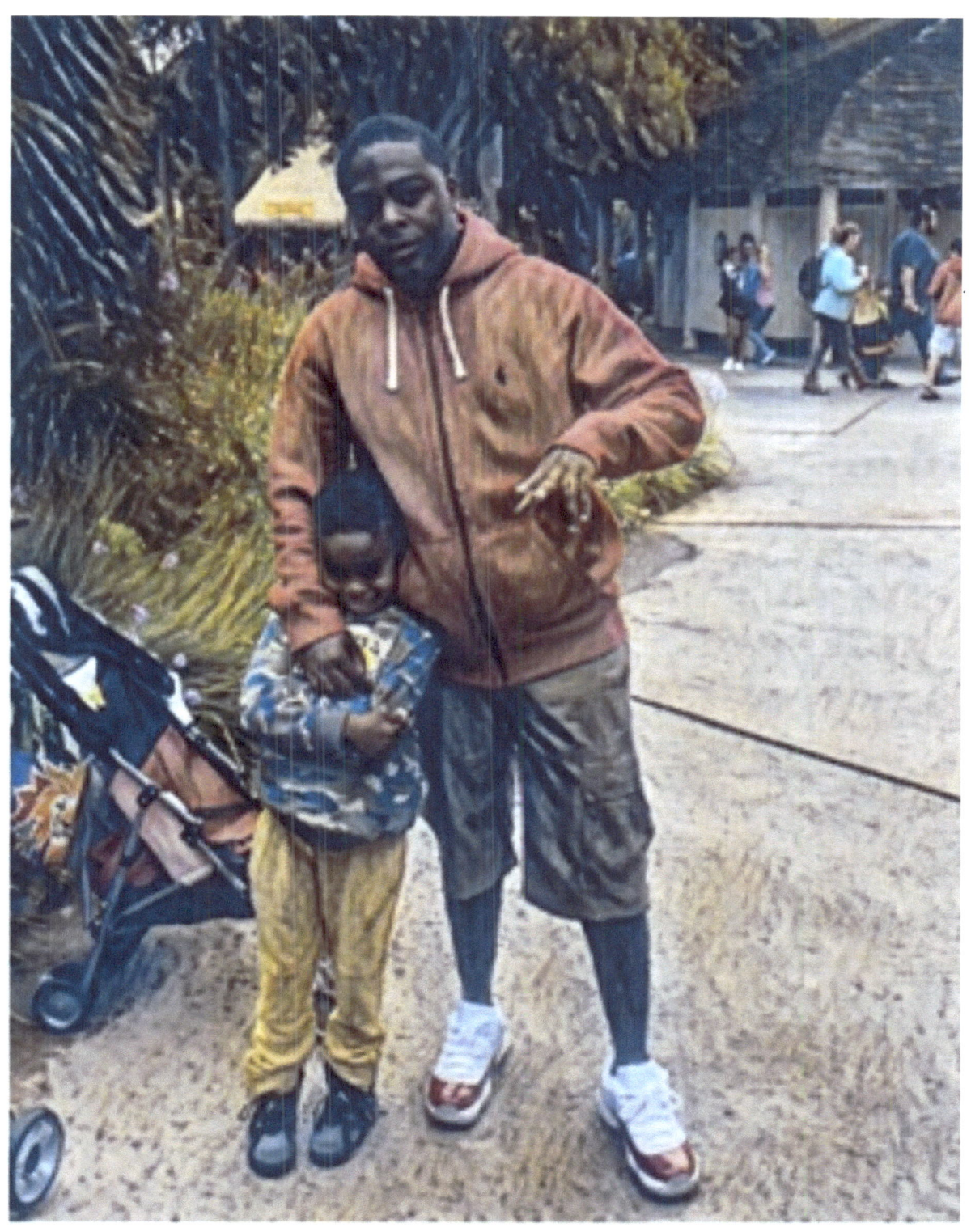

Bonding

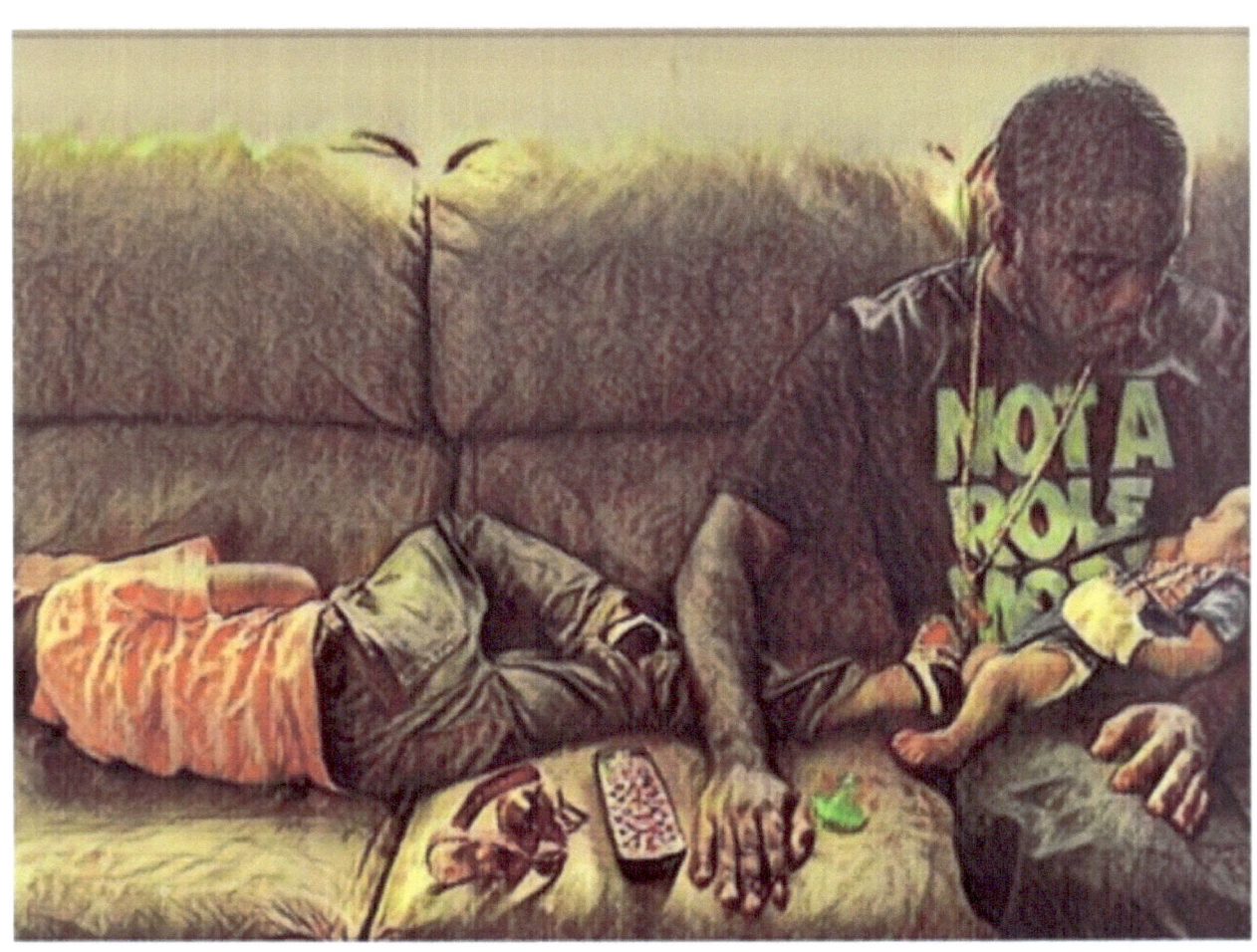

This is what life is all about my two kings

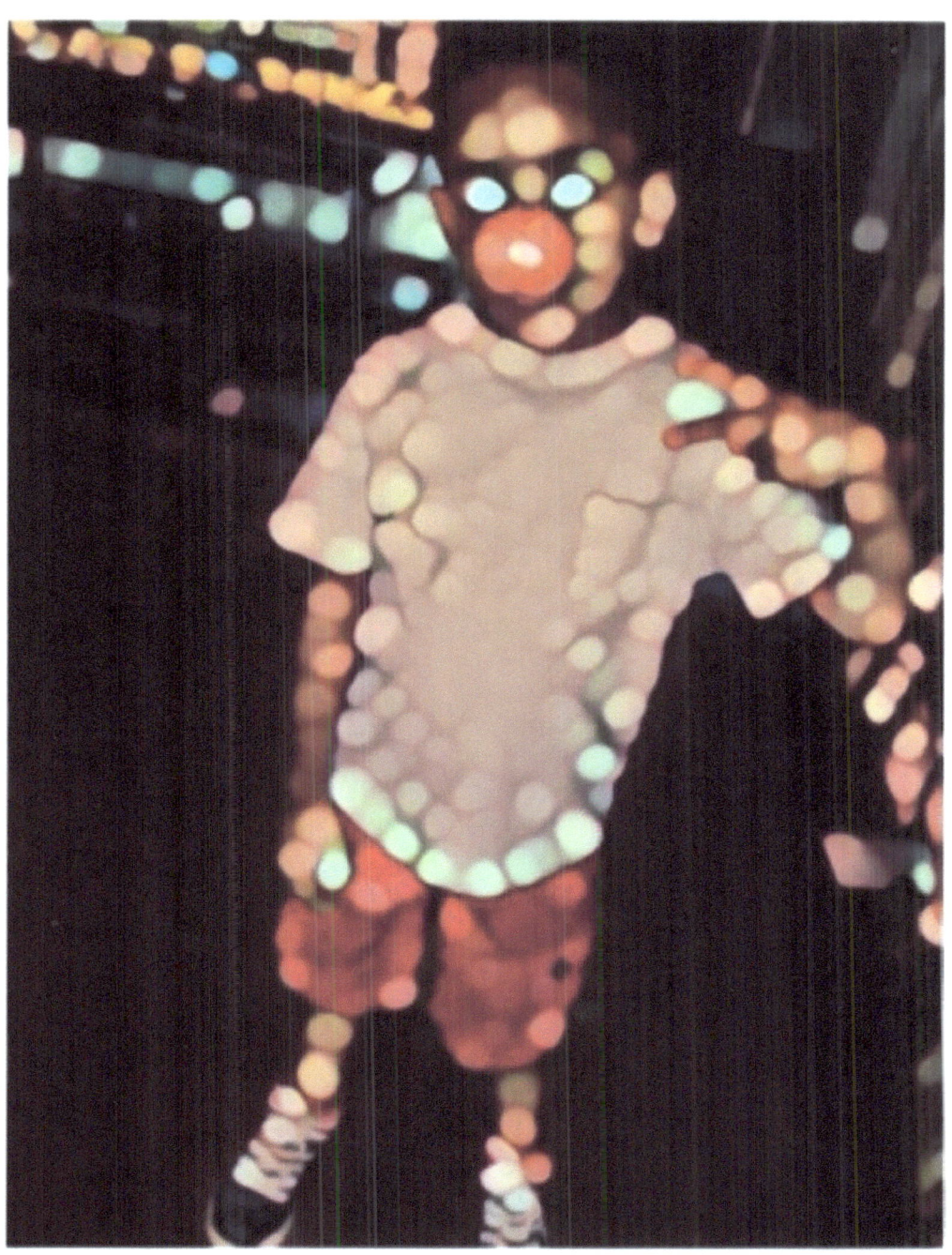

Red nose reindeer

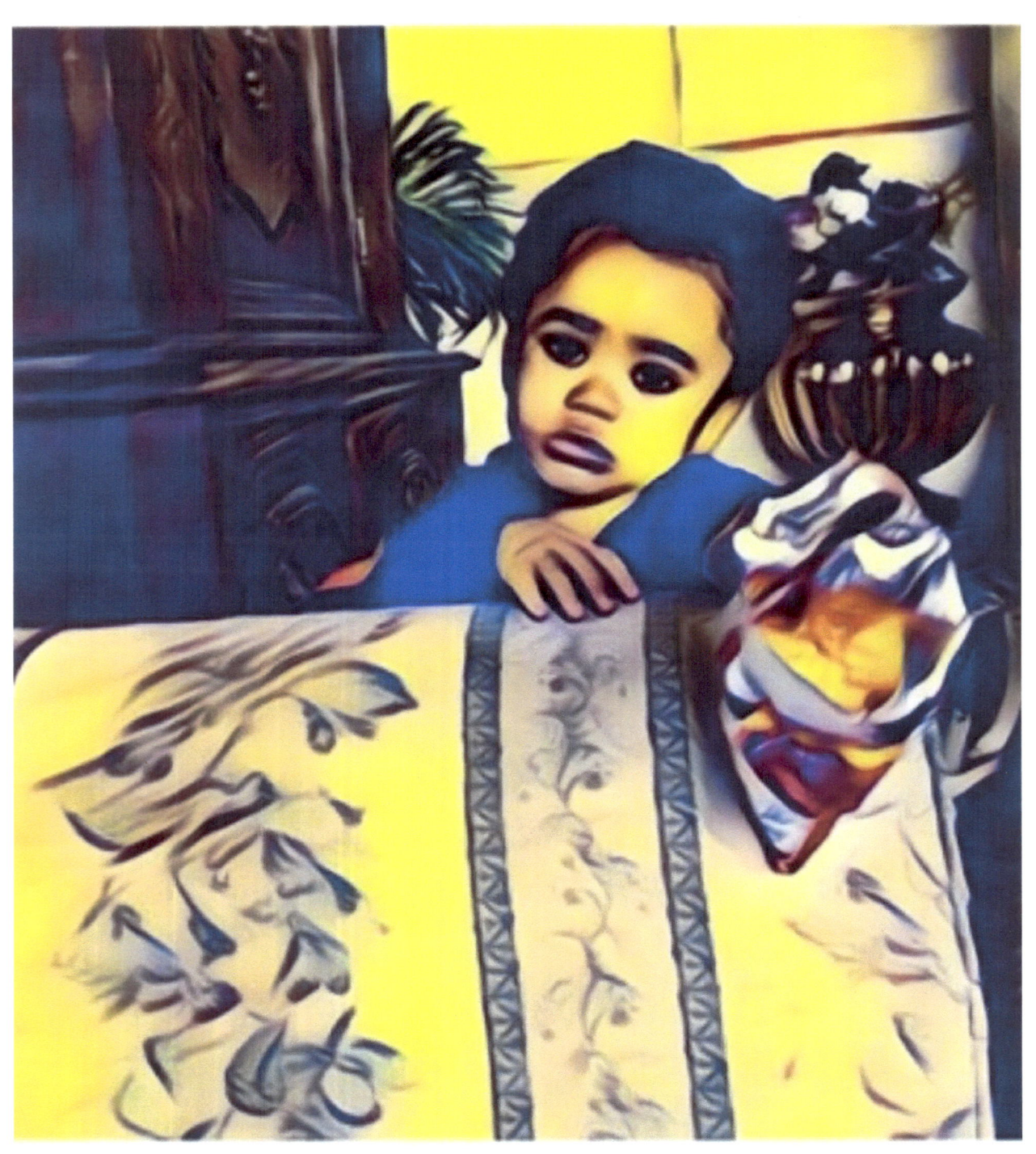

But I don't want to share with anyone

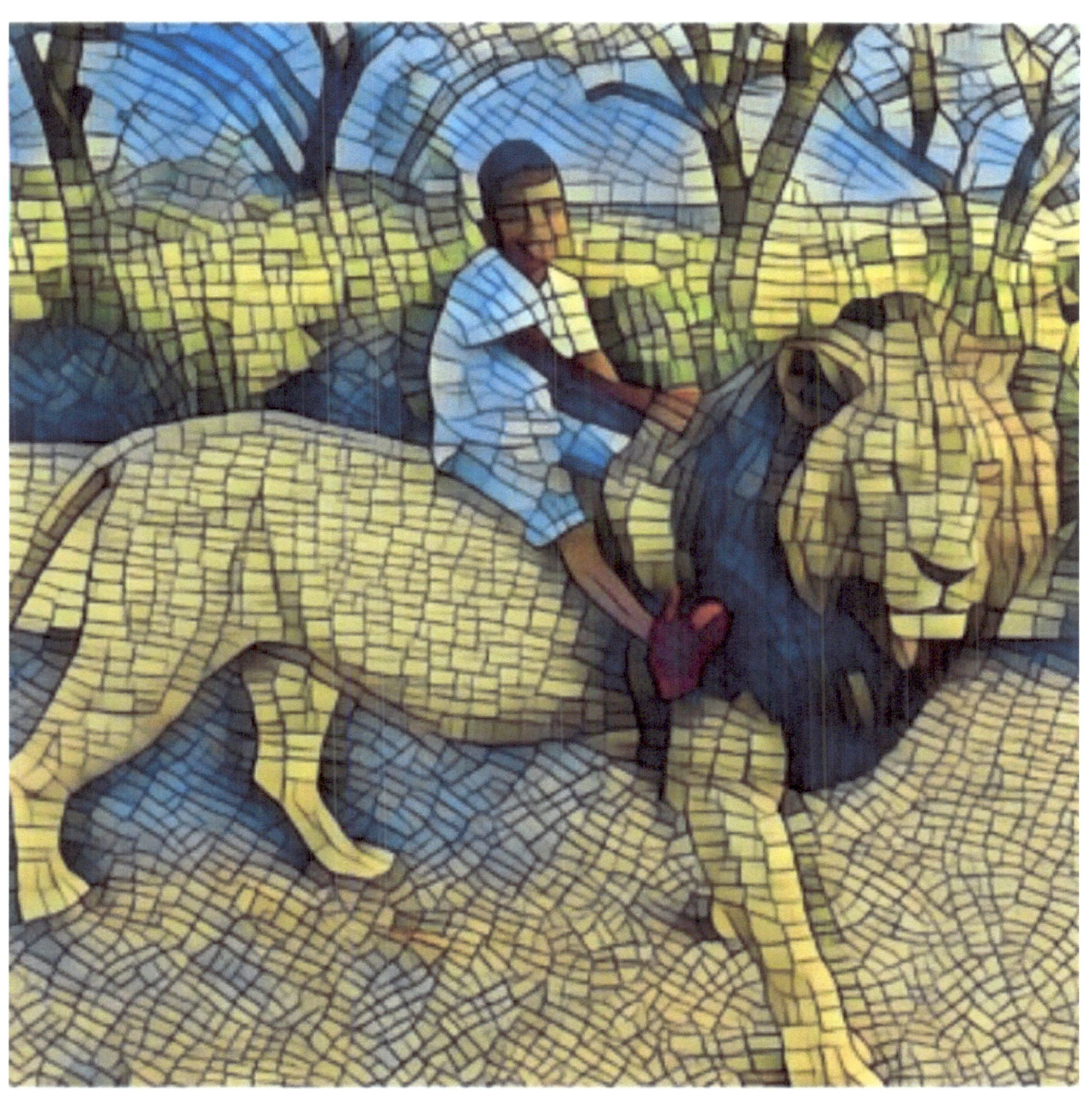

I'm the king of the jungle

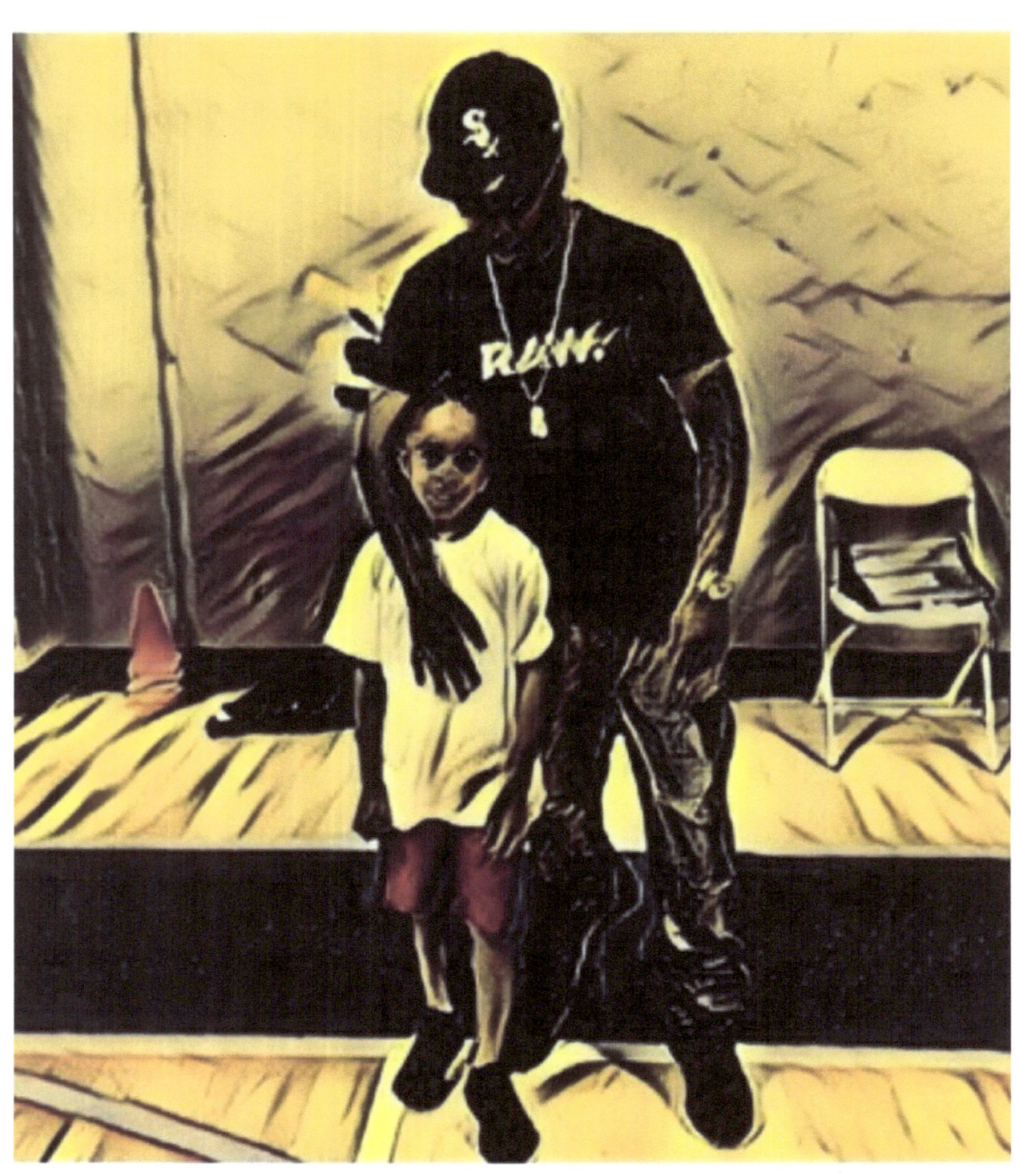

We're attached literally

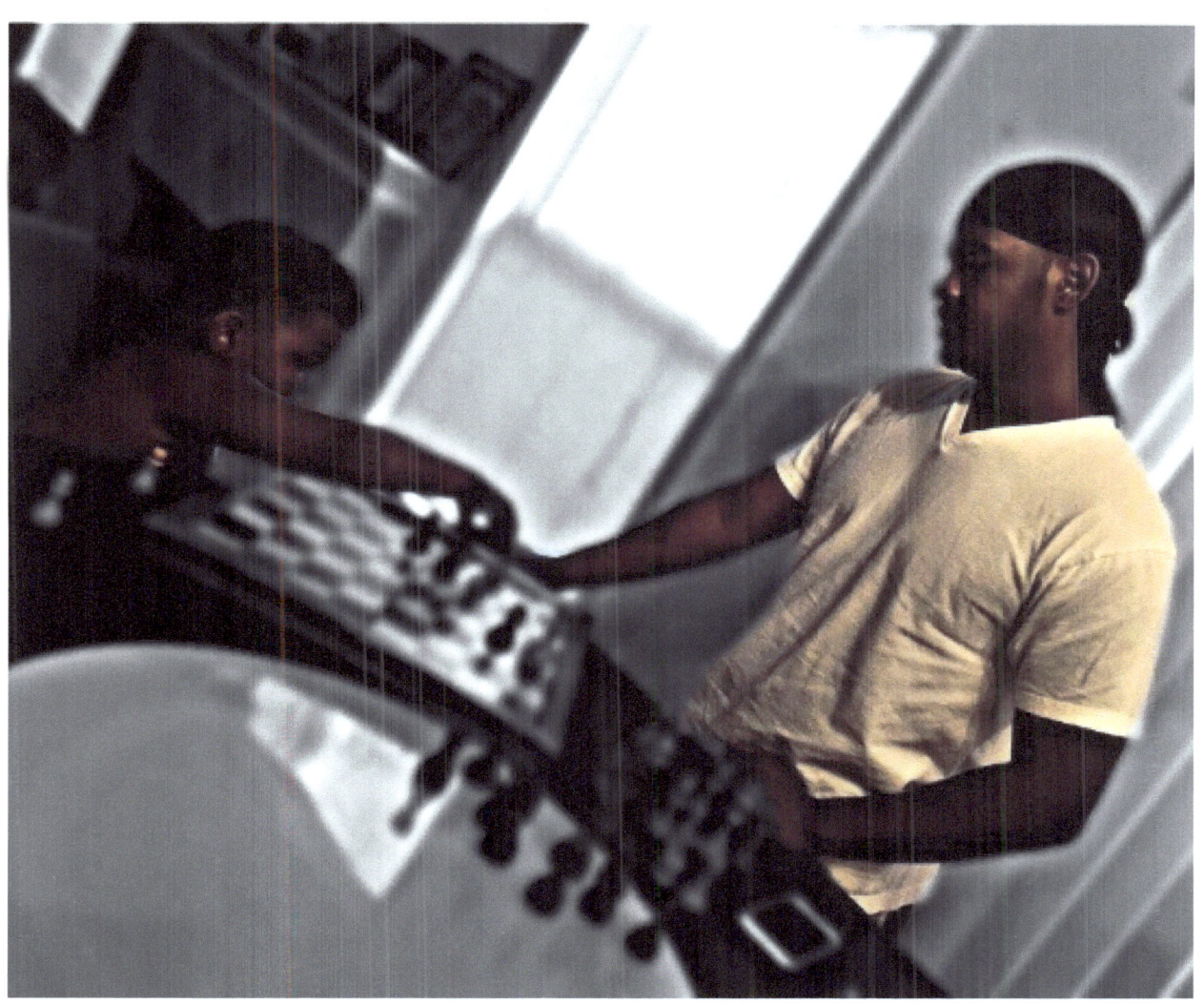

Life is like a game of chess son always remember that

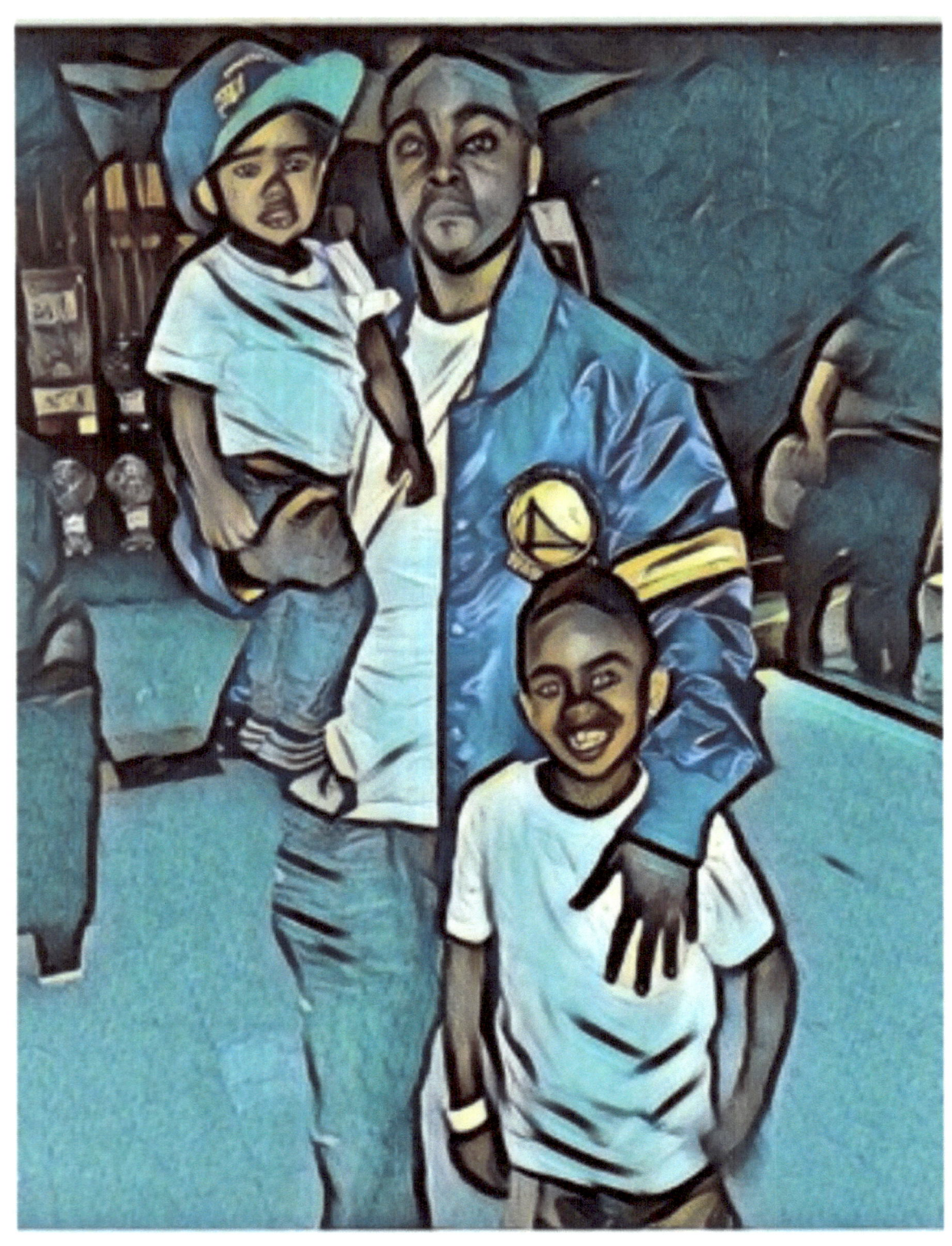

Squad goals

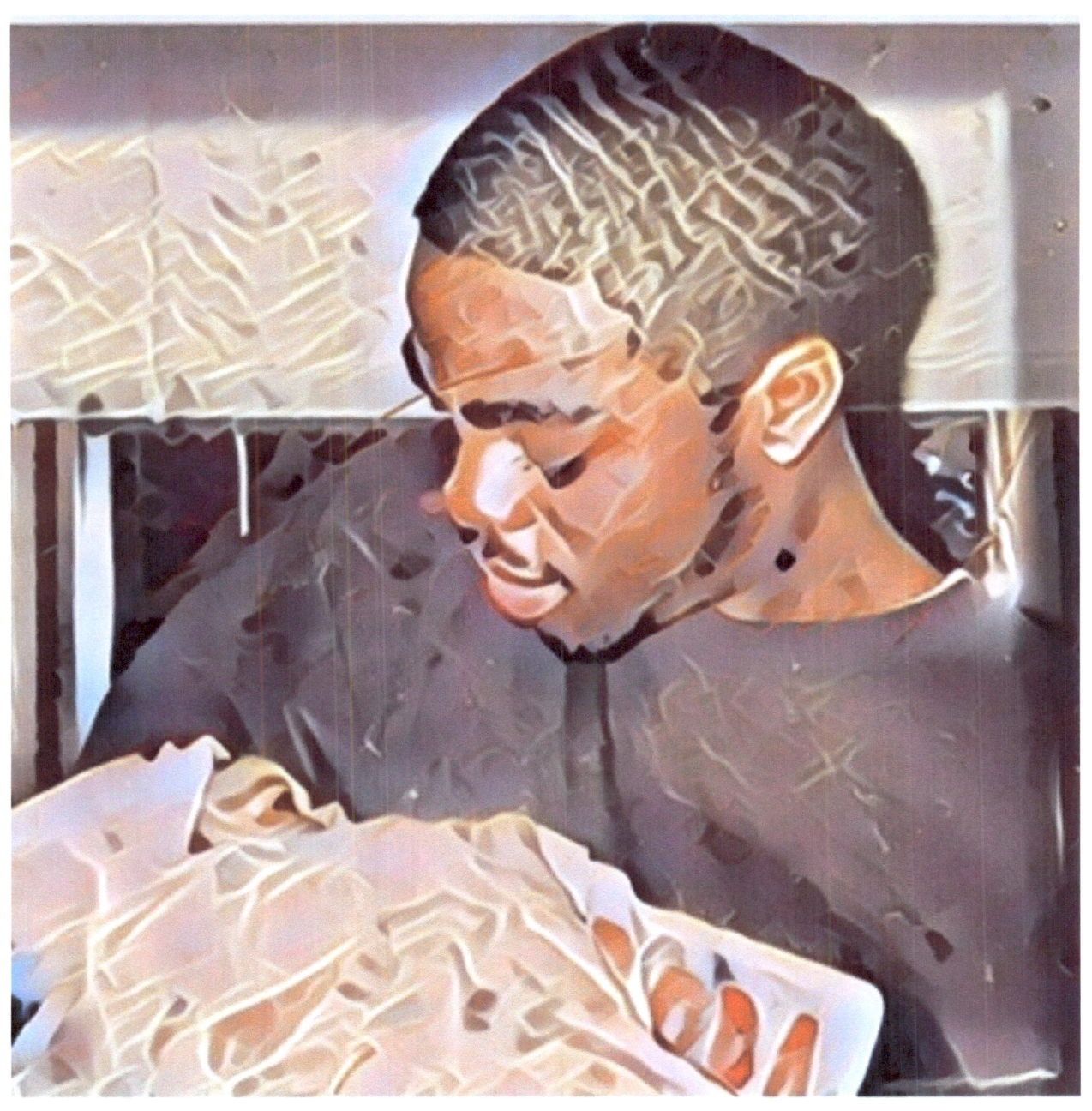

You changed me son Thank God I'm so grateful

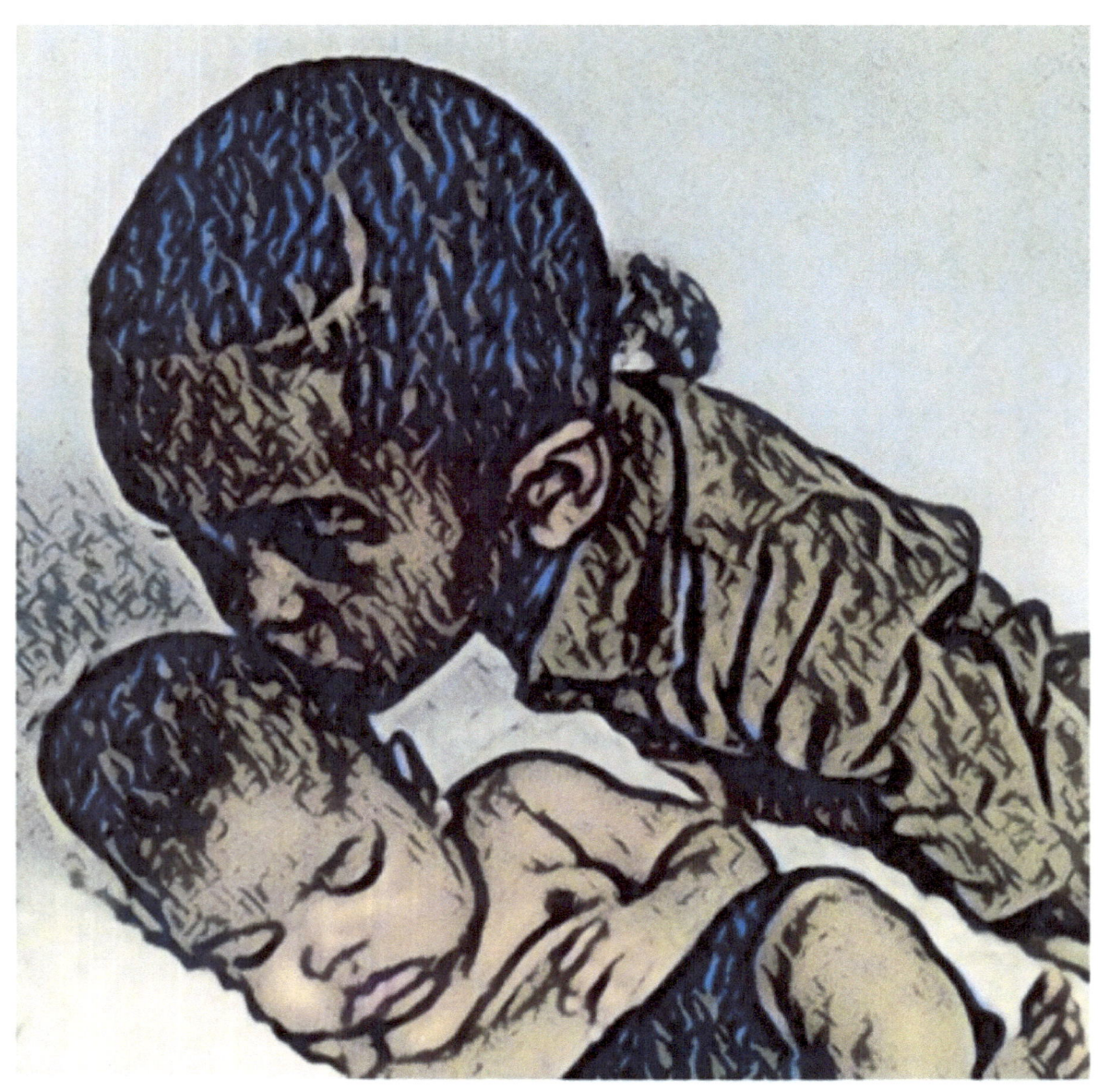

I love you but I didn't know you was going to take all the attention

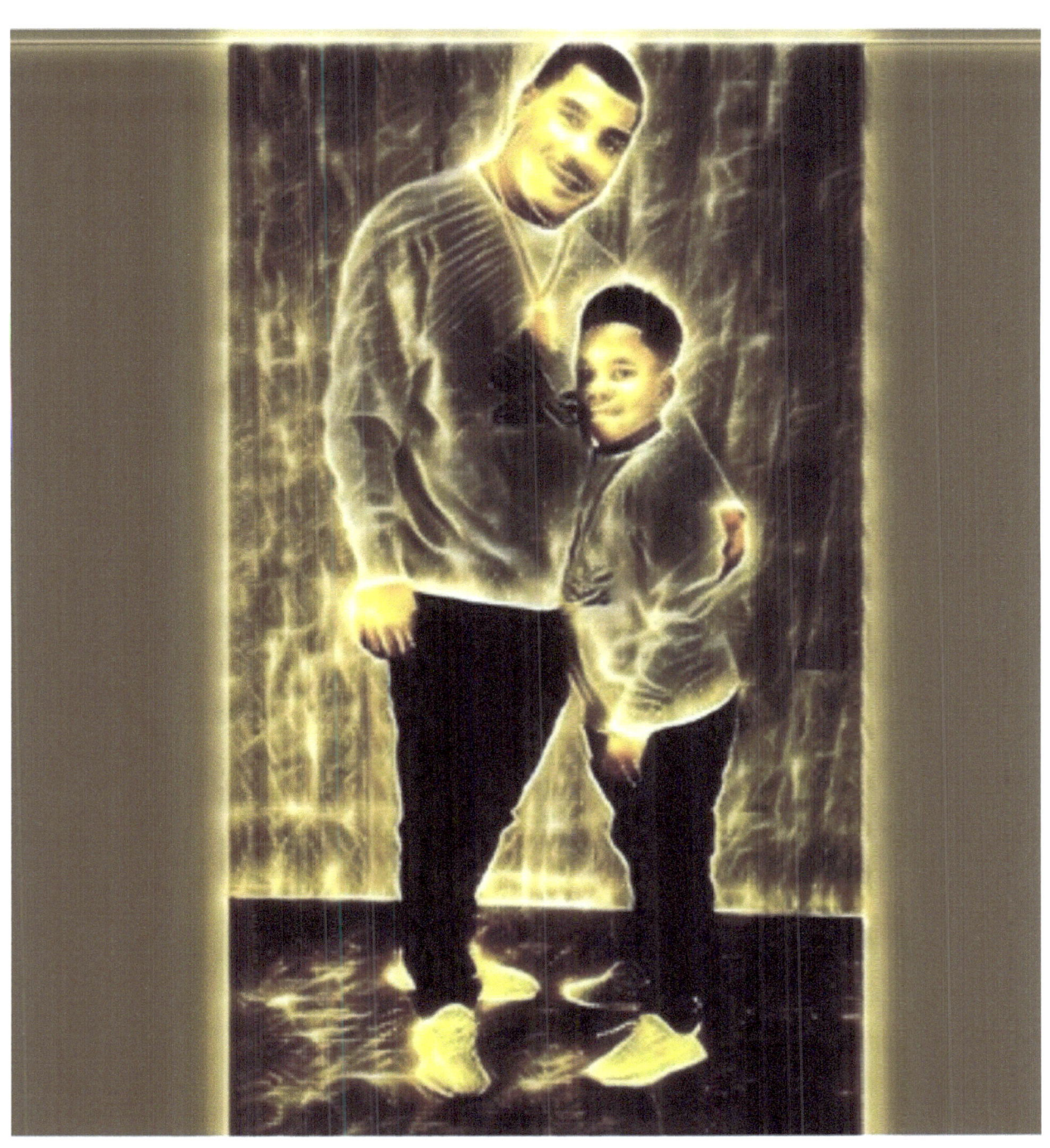

Love unconditional

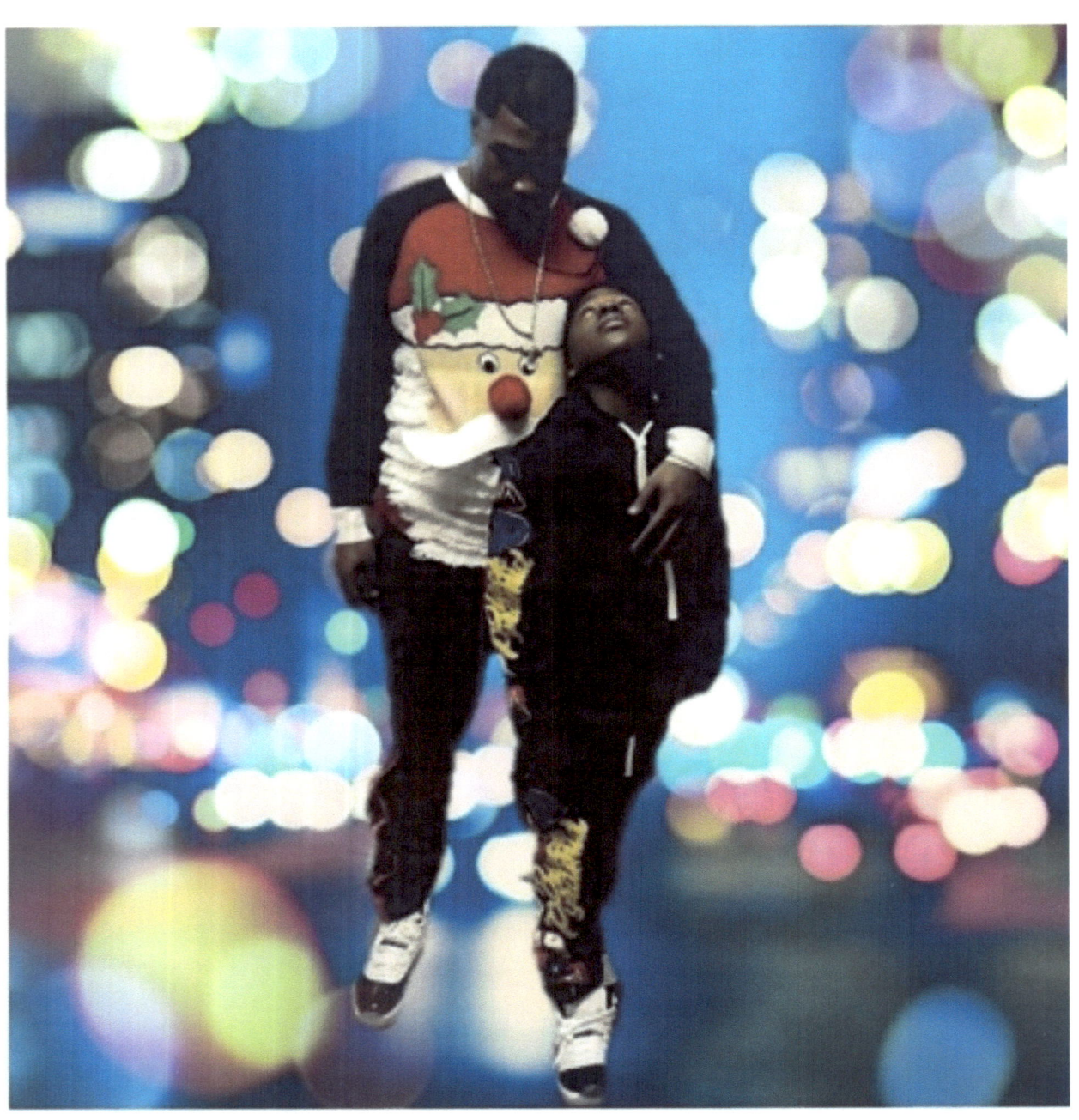

Yeah I'm listening but what are you talking about Dad?

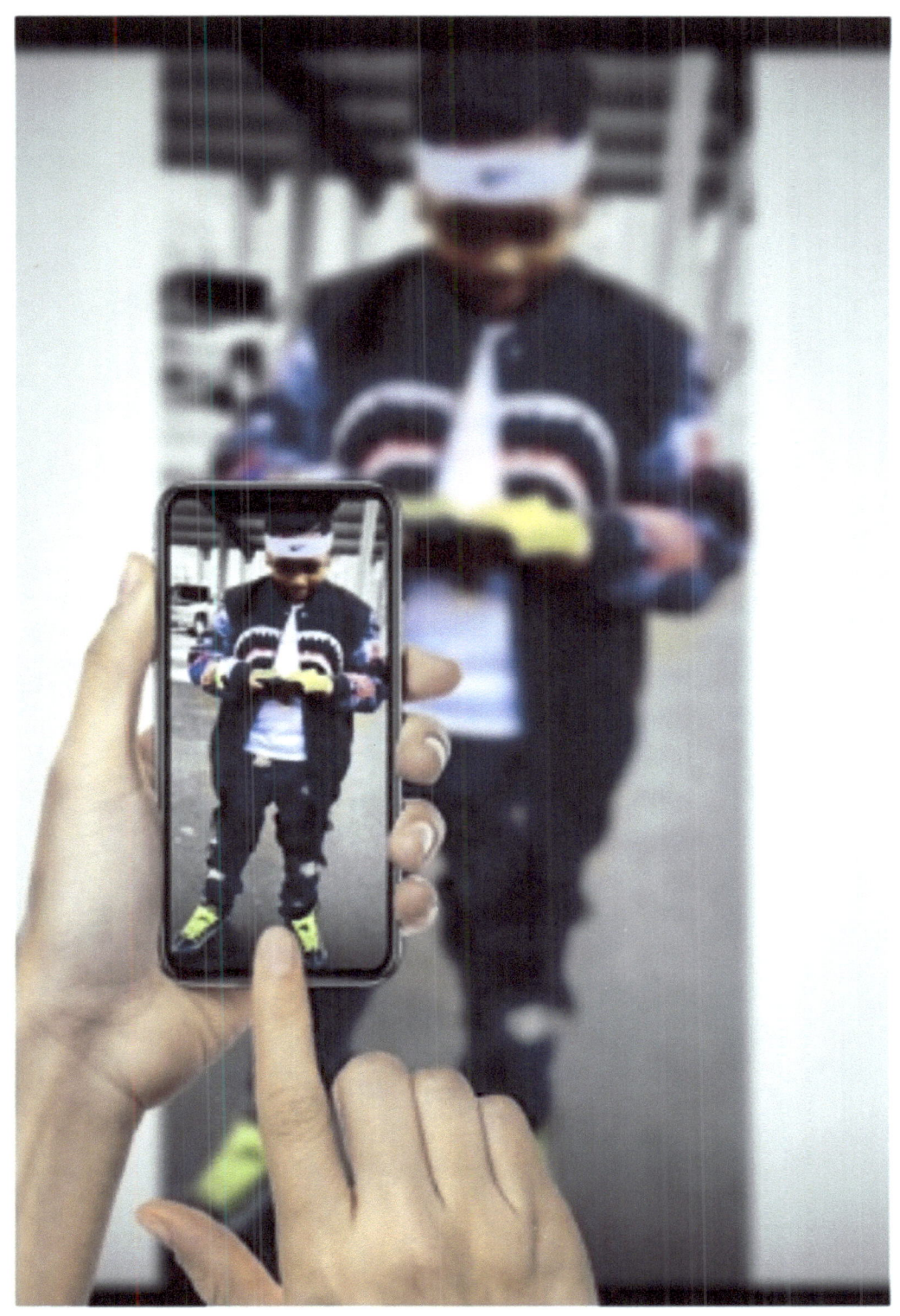

Stay ready so you don't have to get ready

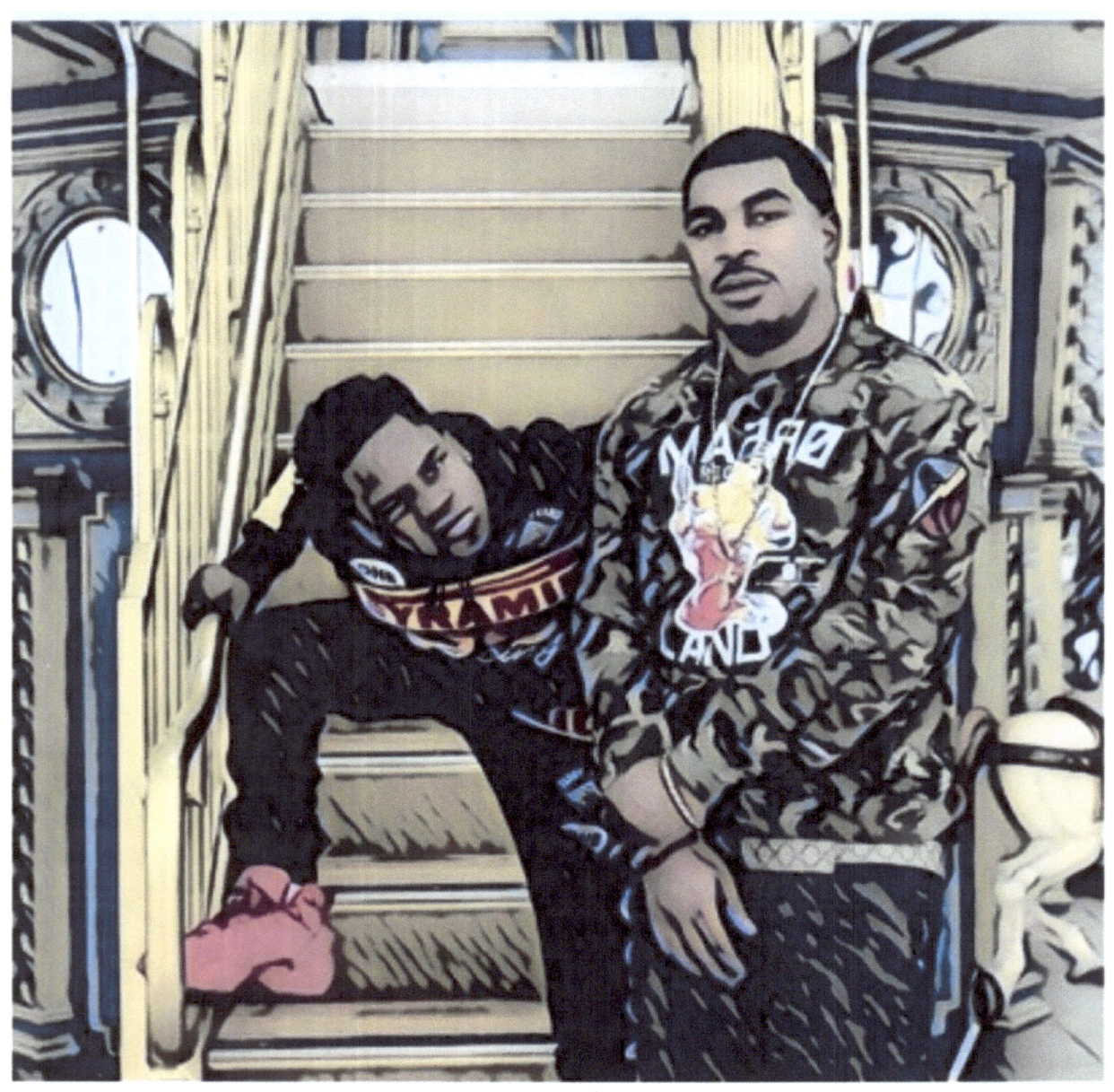

This is us all day me and my daddy

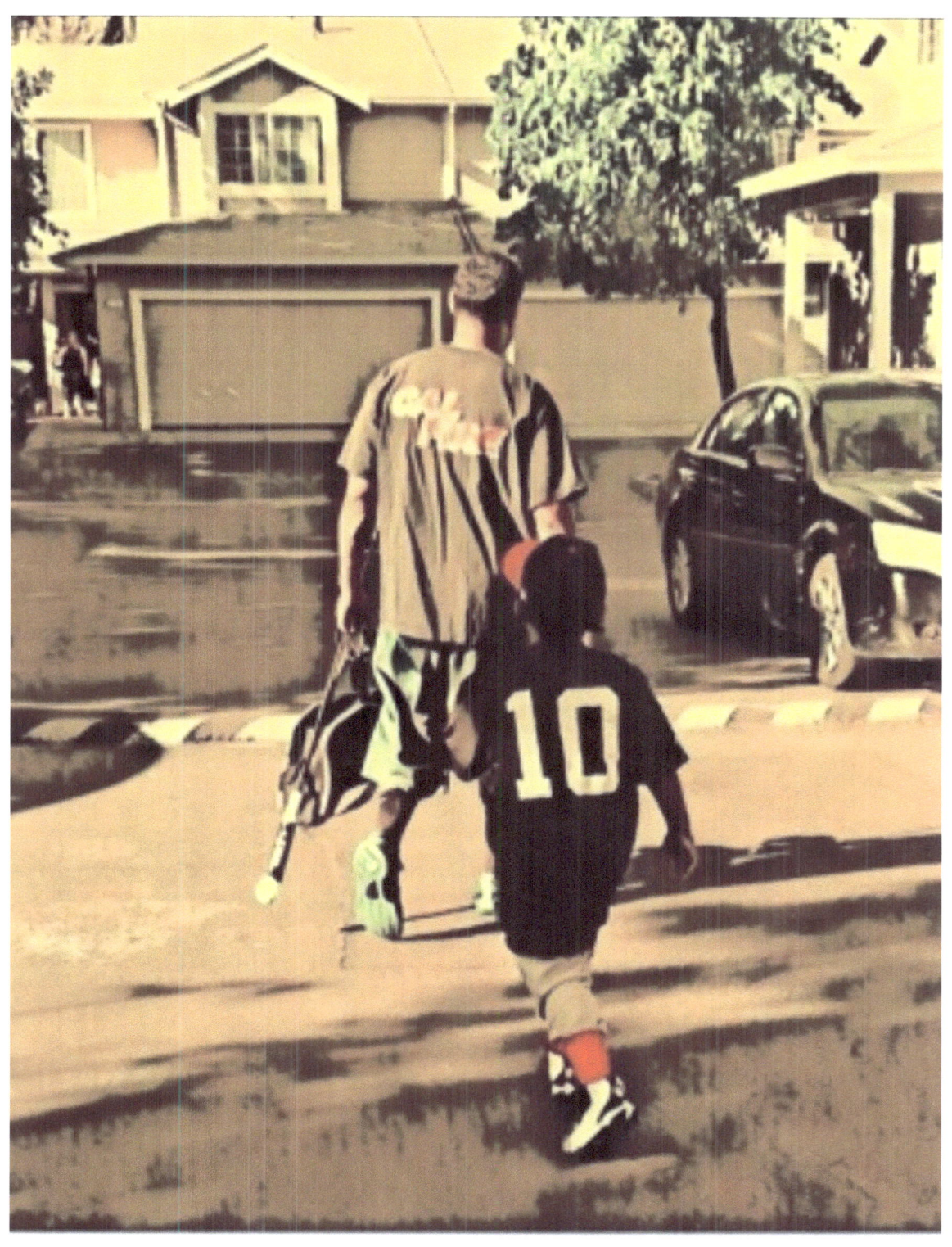

You lead daddy I'll follow you

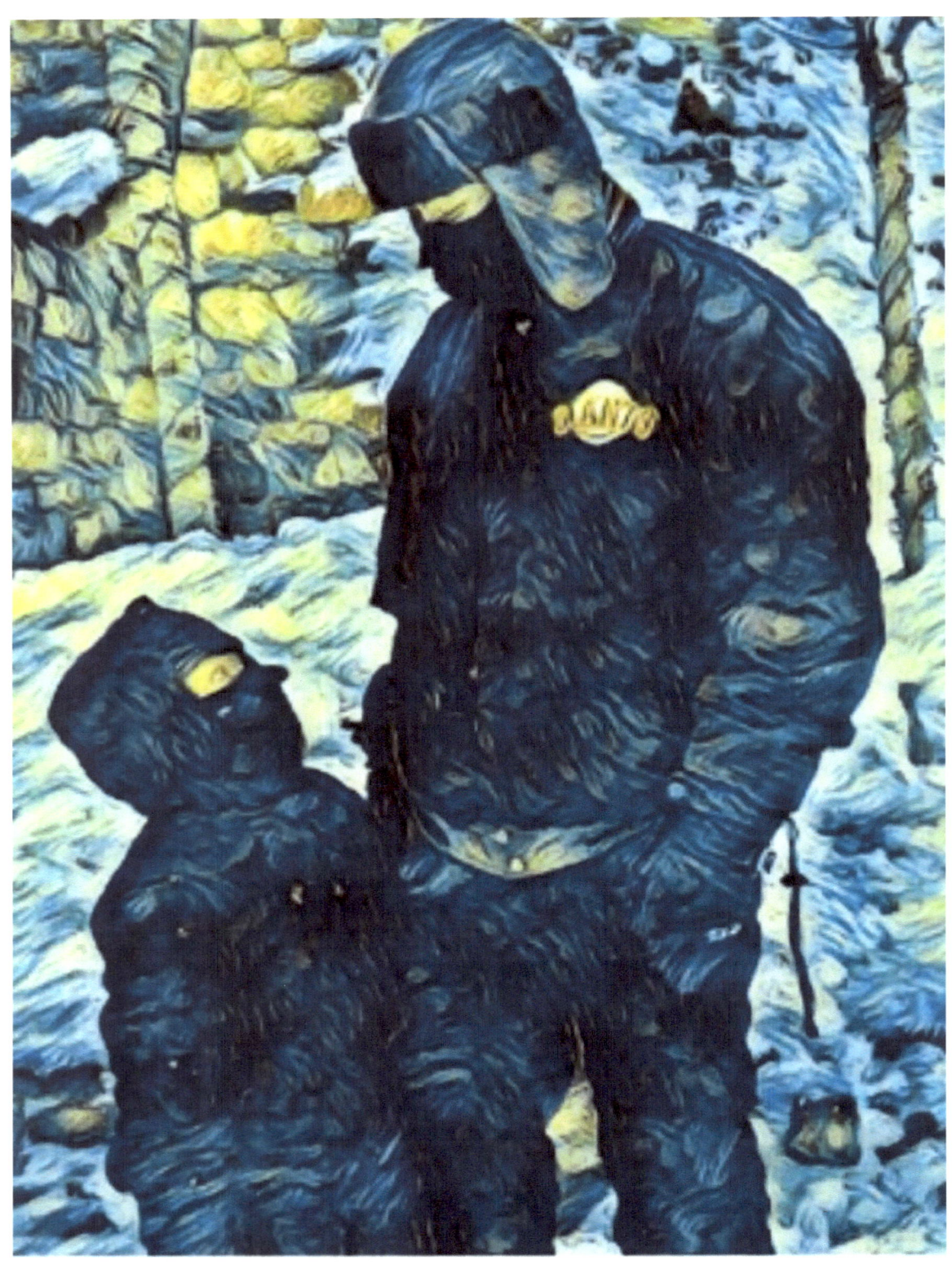

Trust me son when I tell you I got you for life

Authors Dylan, Damare, Devin, Terrell Thank you for your support we love you all. Godbless